Enterta
on a Budget

SARA LEWIS

◆A◆C◆E◆
BOOKS

©1994 Sara Lewis

Published by Age Concern England
1268 London Road
London SW16 4ER

Production Marion Peat
Editors Deborah Murdoch, Odile Hearn
Design and typesetting Eugenie Dodd Typographics
Printed in Great Britain by Bell & Bain Ltd, Glasgow

A catalogue record for this book is available
from the British Library.

ISBN 0–86242–147–0

Contents

ABOUT THE AUTHOR 5

ACKNOWLEDGEMENT 6

AUTHOR'S INTRODUCTION 7

1 Entertaining well 8

A special occasion 9

Care with expense 9

Enjoy yourself 10

Time trimming 10

Time planning 11

Entertaining often 11

2 Party presentation 12

Wine guide 12

Ice magic 13

Floral tribute 13

By candlelight 14

Miniature charm 14

A finishing touch 15

3 How to use the recipes 17

Cost 17

Quantity control 18

Be prepared 18

Adapting the recipes 18

Your choice 19

4 The menus   20

Key to the recipe symbols   20

Birthday celebration for six   21
Bistro supper for six   26
Chinese supper for six   30
Curry supper for four   35
Easy Italian supper for four   40
Family Sunday lunch for six   43
Freeze-ahead dinner for six   49
Greek-style supper for four   54
Saturday brunch for six   58
Slow-cook supper for six   61
Speedy supper for six   63
Quick meat-free supper for four   66
Smart vegetarian dinner for four   69
Alfresco lunch for four   74
Picnic lunch for six   77
Summer barbecue party for six   81
Store cupboard supper for four   85
Harvest supper for six   89
'Best of British' supper for six   95
Bonfire night party for eight   99
Winter warming dinner for six   103
Christmas drinks and nibbles
party for eight   107
Christmas Eve supper for four   112
Traditional Christmas lunch for
eight   115
New Year's Eve dinner for six   124

ABOUT AGE CONCERN   129
PUBLICATIONS FROM ACE BOOKS   130
INDEX TO THE RECIPES   134

About the author

Sara Lewis is a cookery journalist and a qualified home economist; she is freelance cookery editor on *Practical Parenting* magazine and contributes regularly to women's magazines. She has two small children. She was formerly cookery editor of *Family Circle* magazine and her great love is to cook for family and friends. She is the author of *Eating Well on a Budget*, also published by ACE Books.

Acknowledgement

A special thank you to my husband Andrew for always making friends and family so welcome when entertaining.

Sara Lewis
July 1994

Author's introduction

Going out for a meal with friends is one of the nicest ways to spend an evening, but it can prove expensive and sometimes disappointing. So it makes sense to entertain at home, where you have complete control over the choice and quality of the meal, and also the cost.

This book aims to show you how extraordinarily cost-effective, easy and worthwhile entertaining can be. One party meal costs only 75p per guest and many cost only about £1 per head. The book includes over 100 delicious but inexpensive recipes in 25 specially planned menus. These are designed to cover many different occasions throughout the year, ones which deserve to be marked by a special meal and celebrated with friends around you. There is a wide variety of menus to choose from: recipes for vegetarian friends; quick delicious meals to rustle up when time is short; meals for guests who enjoy exotic dishes and menus for those with more traditional tastes. In addition, there are menus for the most important days of the year in terms of special meals: Christmas and New Year.

Each recipe has useful tips attached to help even the novice cook feel relaxed and confident and to let experienced cooks see where there is scope for variation and special decorative effects. But first, the introductory chapters deal with the background information you need to help you go about entertaining in a more positive, better-informed way, with the aim that the cook, too, will find it more enjoyable.

Sara Lewis

Sara Lewis

1 Entertaining well

Entertaining – a lovely adjective to apply to anyone – means warm, witty, friendly, relaxed. But does your attitude change when it comes to using the word as a noun – when you think of entertaining as a task you have to take on? Some people reaching retirement age may want to take life a little easier; they may also feel less strong and energetic than they once were, and, as a result, less inclined to entertain as often. Though it may seem tiring to cook for guests as well as yourself, the psychological benefits are considerable.

- One in four people live alone and eating a solitary meal can be a hurried, demoralising affair.
- Couples, too, will reap the benefit of more varied social contacts at meal times. It's very easy for even a wonderfully close relationship to become inward-looking when couples are solely dependent on each other for day-to-day companionship – little habits can become intensely irritating, the other person's responses annoyingly predictable.

You might feel you don't want to be bothered with the demands and expectations of formal entertaining, but making a deliberate effort to include others in your life by inviting them for a meal as often as possible helps keep you in touch and keeps you outward-looking. With the increase in depressive illness in this country over recent years, it's worth remembering that entertaining can actually be therapeutic.

A special occasion

Does entertaining have to be formal? General trends have been towards greater informality – and that does not have to mean a decline in standards. The things which make a meal special aren't necessarily expensive ingredients and finest wines. A meal can be special purely because the event is linked to a special date in the calendar – Harvest Festival, New Year's Day, Sunday lunch. The food need not be costly when the timing of the invitation can make the occasion fun and memorable. Your invitation might, for instance, be: 'It's Chinese New Year, come round for a Chinese meal.' Nor need entertaining always mean eating formally indoors – many guests will be delighted to be invited round for a barbecue, or an alfresco picnic. In all these cases the ingredients can be inexpensive and the cooking easy – it is the planning of something different which gives style and flair to the invitation and makes it an entertaining prospect.

Care with expense

However carefully someone shops normally, however keenly they usually track down bargains, all that can change when friends have been asked round for a meal. Quite simply, it doesn't seem right not to 'treat' guests to the best of everything. This can be a reason for holding back from entertaining – it is just too expensive to spend lavishly on party meals more than a few times a year. So it is worthwhile asking if this is really necessary. Does party food always have to be expensive, elaborate food?

Thinking back to really pleasurable meals at friends' houses, do we remember the food in detail, or isn't it rather the talk, the laughter, the good feeling of being with people we like which is most memorable? It can surely be argued that the art of good entertaining is to make sure that the party food is carefully gauged to be unobtrusively excellent – rather than stunningly conversation stopping.

In collecting the recipes for this book, the aim has been to take the worry out of entertaining. There are brief time plans to help answer the question: 'How will we cope with talking to guests and get things in and out of the oven at the right moment?' Every cook, and certainly all expert ones, ask themselves this – so you'll see that planning ahead is worthwhile even when cooking very quick meals.

Enjoy yourself

Another tip from expert cooks is to choose dishes which are well within your ability when entertaining. If you set your sights too high, choosing elaborate recipes from the great restaurant chefs, for instance, there is a danger of losing the enjoyment of the party yourself because you will have to devote so much time and effort to the cooking. Once we can get rid of this stressful idea and instead try other ways of giving a good dinner party – and they do exist – there is a chance of finding a new pleasure in entertaining.

Time trimming

One of the most time-consuming elements of entertaining is choosing and balancing the recipes for the complete meal. All the recipes in this book are presented with entertaining in mind and are linked to form complete menus. This, again, is intended to contribute towards making even a simple, budget-conscious meal a special one. For it is possible to spend a lot of money on food but then balance the menu badly so that, for instance, guests find themselves eating a cream soup, a main course in a creamy sauce, then a creamy pudding. However expensive the ingredients involved, guests won't enjoy a meal like that; not only will the colour of the various dishes be monotonous but the guests' palates will not be tempted by varied tastes. A meal which is special will have the flavours, textures and colours of the different dishes constantly varied.

The chapter on 'Party presentation' gives more hints on making the table look beautiful too; for the visual appeal of food matters a great deal and the anticipation felt when guests sit down to an imaginatively laid table is a great appetiser!

Time planning

The truly entertaining hosts are ones who put delicious food before you with apparent ease and have ample time to talk over it. Imagine yourself as a guest for a moment, seeing the cook flustered and preoccupied, or absent for long spells in the kitchen – how do you feel? Does it inevitably diminish your enjoyment of the party? Most of us would rather eat a simple, delicious dish with friends often, than see them only occasionally because 'a dinner party is such a lot of work'.

There are two ways to cut down on work on the day:

■ Cook as much as possible beforehand – make use of the freezer when it won't impair flavour or texture, or a slow cooker if you have one. This book gives notes on when this is possible.

■ Choose fast-to-make recipes which are so simple that you can cook succeeding courses quickly.

Entertaining often

The more often you cook for guests the less work it becomes. This is a theory which you can test for yourself. Arrange to have people round for meals on two occasions in quick succession, allowing only a full day or a couple of days in between. The second occasion will be vastly simpler! Your flowers, as long as they were carefully chosen, will last from the first party and will only need fresh water; your glasses, cutlery, dinner service and so on are all to hand and freshly washed instead of being packed away in remote cupboards! Some ingredients – egg whites for instance, dressing for salad, pesto sauce or sherry perhaps – will also be to hand from the first party's recipes. But over and above this, you, as cook and party manager will feel in the swing of things. 'Don't let yourself get out of practice' is a good maxim for successful entertaining, even when you are on a tight budget.

2 Party presentation

However tight the budget, allow some money for decorative effects and garnishes when entertaining – it can make all the difference between an ordinary meal and a party one. Laying the table beautifully need not cost much. Try getting out the best china, cutlery and your favourite tablecloth to see how it makes a simple supper into a special occasion. Many of us will agree ruefully that there is little point having lovely china when it languishes in the sideboard most of the year. We should seize more opportunities to let ourselves, and our guests, appreciate it.

The expert's tip is to allow plenty of time to lay the table, well before guests arrive, however fast the cooking of the actual meal is planned to be. Check the tablecloth and napkins are clean and ideally iron any creases out of them. Wipe over placemats, buff up cutlery and polish glasses with a clean, dry tea towel to a sparkling finish.

Wine guide

If serving white wine, don't forget to allow plenty of time for it to chill; even a good white wine can be unpleasant served lukewarm, while a moderately priced wine can be delicious if well chilled. Remember to open red wine and have it at room temperature so it can 'breathe'. Make sure the bottle opener is to hand and provide a separate glass for water – more than one glass at each place setting adds party style.

Ice magic

There are several inexpensive tricks with ice which are effective:

- Rather than buying expensive bottled water, fill a large jug with tap water and add plenty of ice cubes and a few slices of lemon or a sprig of mint.

- Guests are always fascinated by special ice cubes. Make them by putting tiny sprigs of fresh herbs, quartered slices of orange or lemon or whole spices in the ice-tray sections before filling with water and freezing.

- To give grandeur to a special occasion, consider making an ice bowl. Use to serve sorbet, ice cream or just to keep the bottle of white wine cool.

To make a bowl, there is no need to invest in one of the special kits on sale. Take two glass or plastic bowls that will fit one inside the other leaving about a 1in (2.5cm) gap between. Fill gap with cooled, boiled water and tape tops of bowls together so that the rims are level. Decorate according to the season, inserting slices of orange, lemon and lime; or holly leaves, cinnamon sticks, cloves, star anise and cranberries or fresh flowers, herbs and leaves.

Freeze for two days until solid. Take out of freezer, remove tape. Dip bowls in a washing-up bowl half-filled with very hot water. Count to 30, lift out of water and twist off outer bowl, You may need to prise a knife down the inside to loosen. Add a little hot water to the inner bowl, count to 20 then remove bowl. Put ice bowl in the freezer on a plate until needed. Fill with ice cream or sorbet and return to freezer. To serve, stand bowl on a plate to catch any drips. Bowl will stay frozen for about two hours.

Floral tribute

A small arrangement of flowers takes little time or money to provide but contributes enormously to a party meal. Try the effect of some garden flowers or perhaps just variegated leaves in a clear glass vase, or try just a couple of special blooms like roses. Ensure the vase is not too tall. You could float a few flowers or petals in a bowl of water with three or four floating candles. Attractive foliage, berries or coloured leaves add a focal point to the party table and even if you do not possess a garden they can be picked while out walking.

By candlelight

Standard white candles are inexpensive but can be grouped to look effective. The soft, flattering glow of candlelight adds greatly to a party atmosphere. Try these ideas:

- Stand white candles on a plate securing them with a little melted wax and encircle the bases with ivy leaves.
- Fill a small terracotta flowerpot with sand and add candles of differing heights. Tie a length of string around outside of pot and twist lengths of ivy, rosemary and thyme around it.
- Press a block of florists' foam into a terracotta flowerpot, add large, slow-burning candles; secure with a cocktail stick pushed first into bases of candles and then into the foam block. Decorate with dried flowers around base of candles – if you have dried hydrangea heads they are very effective. Tie ribbon around pot.

To avoid accidents, ensure lit candles are never left unattended.

Miniature charm

Providing a cheese course often adds a major expense to a party meal. Try these ideas:

- As the cheese course frequently gets left, buy just two or three or more small pieces of cheese, slice into wedges and arrange fanned out on individual plates. Decorate with sprigs of grapes and a few ivy leaves. Cover with cling film and store in a cool place until required. Serve biscuits in a small basket.

- Serve a hot cheese course instead of a cheese board. Stamp out small rounds of bread from a sliced loaf and toast lightly on both sides. Add a thin slice of goats' cheese to each toast round and set aside until required. When ready to serve, grill until cheese is hot and just melted. Arrange one for each person on individual plates with a little salad garnish. Serve immediately.

A finishing touch

Few people can resist a tiny chocolate or two to go with their coffee, especially if they are home-made. They can be made up when you have time and frozen. Simply take out enough to provide two per person and defrost for one hour when required. Truffles made with cream and a few tablespoons of whatever spirit you have make guests feel they have had a real touch of luxury.

Creamy chocolate truffles

MAKES 30
6oz (150g) deluxe cooking chocolate
¼pt (150ml) double cream
1oz (25g) butter
2tbsp icing sugar

TO FINISH:
4tbsp cocoa powder

1 Break chocolate into pieces and melt in a bowl over a saucepan of hot water.

2 Put cream into a small saucepan, bring just to the boil then take off heat and add butter. Leave until melted.

3 Take bowl of chocolate off saucepan and gradually whisk in cream mixture and icing sugar. Add flavourings – see 'Variations' on next page. Chill overnight in fridge until hard.

4 Take teaspoons of mixture and shape into small balls. Roll in cocoa and chill on a baking sheet lined with greaseproof paper until required.

Variations

BRANDY AND GINGER

Add 2tsp chopped glacé ginger and 2tbsp brandy. Coat in cocoa or 8oz (225g) melted chocolate. Decorate with a tiny piece of ginger.

NUTTY CLUSTERS

Grill 4oz (100g) blanched hazelnuts or almonds until lightly browned. Roughly chop and stir into truffle mixture. Dip truffles in 8oz (225g) melted chocolate and swirl with a fork.

IRISH COFFEE

Add 1tsp coffee granules and 2tbsp whisky to truffle mixture. Roll in sifted icing sugar or cocoa.

To freeze, open freeze on a baking sheet until hard then pack into a plastic box, interleaving layers with greaseproof paper. Seal, label and freeze for up to 3 months. Defrost at room temperature for 1 hour. Dust with extra cocoa or icing sugar if needed.

How to use the recipes 3

Cost

Each of the menus on the following pages has been costed to fall within one of three price categories; prices are for whole menus and symbols appear at the start of each menu to indicate the cost. Details of the symbols are given on page 20. Ten recipes are in the cheapest category (£), which is under £7 (from 75p to £1.62 a head). Around half of the menus are in the mid-range category (££) and are under £10 (under £2 a head). There are just three recipes in the most expensive category (£££), under £18; these serve eight people and are still only a little over £2 a head. The Christmas lunch is the most expensive, working out at around £2.25 a head (£18 for eight) but the quantities given will mean plenty of turkey left over for further meals.

The majority of costs were calculated using current supermarket prices except where market prices for basic vegetables and fruit were used. They were correct at time of going to press (August 1994). Prices may, of course, vary according to the season in which a particular recipe is used and where ingredients are bought. You will find tips on when it is most cost-effective to buy from market stalls or supermarkets and the recipes will also direct you when appropriate towards the very keen prices to be found at freezer centres. When fresh fruit and vegetables are needed, it is, in general, cheaper to buy at open markets and advisable to go to one or two stalls you know you can trust.

Quantity control

It is important to choose whether to use imperial or metric measurements – not a combination of the two. Please note also that all spoon measures are level and that the recipes have been tested using a set of measuring spoons; these are available at a reasonable price from kitchen shops. If using your own household spoons, remember that these vary considerably in size and may differ greatly from standard measuring spoon sizes.

Be prepared

Some of the recipes use ingredients which most people are likely to have in store, whether dry goods or cans, vegetables in the rack or food in the fridge. These recipes are very useful to remember when there is suddenly an opportunity to entertain guests – you can invite them to join you for a 'pot luck' supper. You will find a symbol for store-cupboard ingredients (see page 20) beside these recipes and you may like to look out for them when first reading through the recipes so you can turn to them quickly when the occasion arises.

Adapting the recipes

There is no need to follow the ingredients suggested in every respect. Many items, such as frozen meats for instance, are specified simply because they are much cheaper. If it is more convenient to use fresh meat and you can budget for the extra expense, by all means do; if you have a good butcher you will usually find the taste is better, although when cooking a highly spiced dish the difference may not be noticeable. Similarly, dried or frozen herbs are sometimes specified because fresh ones may not be available. The taste of fresh herbs is far better and they make a very important contribution to delicious dishes. It is much cheaper to grow your own herbs and use these if possible.

Margarine has been specified in many recipes because it is cheaper and because anyone trying to cut down on dairy fats for health reasons may prefer to use it as it is made from vegetable oils. Again, you can substitute butter if you prefer.

In other cases you will find no difference to the excellence of the finished dish when using the budget ingredient suggested; whipping cream for instance is cheaper than double but when whisked up is barely distinguishable. 'Optional' has been marked by some ingredients or garnishes when they have been included to add a stylish touch to the recipe but you can choose to omit them or use favourite garnishes of your own.

Your choice

The recipes are presented as complete menus. There are menus for different seasons of the year and they are balanced to give plenty of variety – they also include recipes for appropriate vegetable dishes and garnishes. Naturally, you can pick and choose between different menus if you are a creative cook. While all the complete menus are listed in the Contents pages, please note that if you are looking for a particular recipe you will find it in the index (pages 134 to 136).

4 The menus

Key to the recipe symbols

PRICE PER MENU

| £ | Budget beater (under £7) | £ £ | Well priced (under £10) | £ £ £ | Low price luxury (under £18) |

Recipe that is quick to prepare and cook

Cooking method

Freezer information

Shopping tip

Ingredients tip

Uses store cupboard ingredients

Nutritional information, including suitability for a vegetarian

Suggestion for varying ingredients, equipment or cooking methods

Tip which gives the expert way

Birthday celebration for six

M E N U   *Chilled cucumber soup*

Honeyed noisettes of lamb with rosemary
Sesame potatoes
Hot bean salad

££   *Strawberry shortcakes*

Chilled cucumber soup

1 small onion, peeled	1pt (600ml) vegetable stock
1 large cucumber, washed	¼pt (150ml) milk
1oz (25g) margarine	6oz (150g) natural yogurt
1oz (25g) plain flour	

1 Chop onion. Cut off and set aside a 1in (2.5cm) thick slice of cucumber. Peel half the remainder then roughly chop all cucumber apart from slice set aside.

2 Heat margarine in a saucepan, add onion and fry for 5 minutes until soft. Add chopped cucumber, stir until coated, cover and cook for 2 minutes. Stir in flour then add stock and seasoning.

3 Bring to the boil, cover and simmer for 10 minutes. Leave to cool.

4 Liquidise or process until smooth. Pour into a bowl and chill until required.

5 Finely chop reserved cucumber. Stir milk and half the yogurt into soup. Ladle into bowls, swirl a little yogurt over top of each and 'feather' with a cocktail stick (pulling outwards at intervals to give a spider's web effect). Sprinkle with chopped cucumber and serve immediately.

Serve soup warm if preferred.

Cucumber skin gives soup its delicate colour but can give a bitter taste – peel away half the skin for good balance between taste and colour.

Use home-made chicken stock or a brand of cubes you know has a good, mild flavour. Do not use strongly seasoned cubes.

Mint can be used
instead of rosemary.

Frozen lamb cutlets
are often the
cheapest buy but they
are very thinly sliced
and therefore too
difficult to shape for
this recipe.

When short of time,
leave bone in chops
and use a stock cube
for sauce.

Honeyed noisettes of lamb with rosemary

12 lamb cutlets	6tbsp red wine or sherry
few sprigs fresh rosemary or 1tsp dried	fresh rosemary to garnish, optional
1tbsp honey	

1 Cut bone away from each cutlet and trim off any excess fat. Curl ends round to make compact, round noisettes. Secure each with 2 cocktail sticks. Season and tuck a small sprig of rosemary into each cutlet or sprinkle with dried rosemary. Put on to a plate, cover and chill until required.

2 Put bones in a saucepan with ¾pt (450ml) water and seasoning. Bring to boil, cover and simmer for 1 hour. Strain and reserve stock.

3 Put cutlets on grill rack and cook under a preheated grill for 4–6 minutes until fat has browned. Turn over, brush with honey and cook for 4–6 minutes.

4 Pour grill pan juices into a saucepan, add wine or sherry and ¼pt (150ml) reserved lamb stock. Bring to boil and simmer for 2–3 minutes until reduced slightly.

5 Meanwhile, remove cocktail sticks from lamb, put on to warmed serving plates and garnish with fresh rosemary, if using. Serve with hot sauce.

Sesame potatoes

1½lb (675g) new potatoes, scrubbed

2tbsp sesame seeds

1oz (25g) margarine

¼tsp paprika

Stir sesame seeds constantly while frying to prevent burning.

1 Halve any large potatoes and cook in a saucepan of boiling salted water for 15 minutes until tender. Drain.

2 Dry pan, add sesame seeds and dry fry until lightly browned. Add margarine and potatoes, and toss together. Spoon into a warmed serving dish and sprinkle with paprika.

Choose small even-sized potatoes so they will all be done at the same time.

Hot bean salad

4oz (100g) French beans, trimmed

8oz (225g) courgettes, trimmed

1 small onion, peeled

2 sprigs fresh rosemary or ¼tsp dried

8oz (225g) tomatoes

1tbsp oil

10oz (283g) can broad beans, drained

Use 1lb (450g) fresh broad beans when in season. Hull and cook with French beans.

1 Halve French beans, thickly slice courgettes. Finely chop onion, strip rosemary leaves from stem and cut tomatoes into wedges. Put aside on a plate until ready to cook.

Quick to make.

2 Cook French beans in a saucepan of boiling salted water for 3 minutes. Add courgettes and cook for a further 3 minutes.

3 Drain beans and courgettes and dry pan. Heat oil, add onion and fry for 3 minutes, add rosemary, tomatoes and broad beans and cook for 2 minutes. Stir in French beans and courgettes, toss together and spoon into a warmed serving dish.

Adding vanilla to shortcake means margarine may be used instead of the traditional butter as it disguises the taste.

Shortcakes may be made 2 days in advance and stored in a plastic box, or frozen for 2 months.

Use other pretty leaves, such as nasturtium or lemon, geranium, if preferred

Strawberry shortcakes

5oz (125g) plain flour
1oz (25g) cornflour
4oz (100g) margarine
2oz (50g) caster sugar
few drops vanilla essence

TO FINISH
1½lb (675g) strawberries
¼pt (150ml) whipping cream
few drops vanilla essence
icing sugar to dust
few mint leaves, optional

1 Sift flour and cornflour into a bowl, add margarine and rub in with fingertips until fine crumbs form. Stir in sugar and vanilla essence.

2 Squeeze mixture lightly together with hands to form a rough ball. Knead lightly on a floured surface then roll out to the thickness of a 50p piece.

3 Cut 12 3in (7.5cm) rounds with a fluted biscuit cutter and put on a baking sheet, re-rolling trimmings to make enough rounds. Prick each with a fork. Chill for 15 minutes.

4 Preheat oven to 350°F, 180°C, Gas 4. Cook shortcakes for 10–12 minutes until pale golden. Leave on baking sheet until completely cold.

5 Reserving 6 small strawberries for decoration, hull remainder and purée half in a liquidiser or food processor. Press through a sieve and discard seeds.

6 Whip cream and vanilla essence until softly peaking; spoon evenly over half the shortcake bases. Slice remaining hulled strawberries and arrange on top of cream. Cover with remaining shortcake rounds. Dust tops with sifted icing sugar and chill until required.

7 To serve, spoon a little strawberry sauce over half of each plate. Add shortcakes, decorate with reserved whole strawberries and mint leaves, if using.

COUNTDOWN ## In the morning

Make and chill cucumber soup. Shape noisettes. Make lamb stock. Scrub potatoes. Prepare vegetables for the bean salad and put on a plate, cover with cling film and chill until required. Make shortcakes and purée half the strawberries for the sauce.

45 minutes before serving

Whip cream and assemble shortcakes, put back on baking sheet and dust with icing sugar.

20 minutes before serving main course

Cook potatoes. Grill noisettes and make sauce. Cook hot bean salad. Fry sesame seeds and finish potatoes. Keep main course hot while garnishing and eating soup.

Arrange shortcakes on serving plates with sauce just before serving.

Bistro supper for six

Livers should still be just pink in the centre. Don't be tempted to cook right through or they will harden.

A good way to provide iron in the diet.

Quick to make.

Warm chicken liver salad

1lb (450g) frozen chicken livers, just thawed

1 round lettuce

2tbsp oil

2tbsp lemon juice

2oz (50g) butter

2 garlic cloves, crushed

4tbsp cider

1 Put livers into a colander, rinse with cold water and drain well. Cut any large ones in half and discard any green or white parts.

2 Tear lettuce into pieces, rinse with cold water and dry. Put oil, lemon juice and seasoning into a large bowl and whisk together with a fork. Add lettuce and toss. Divide between 6 small plates.

3 Heat butter in a frying pan, add livers, garlic and seasoning and fry for 5 minutes, stirring frequently, until browned but still slightly pink in the centre.

4 Add cider and cook for 1 minute. Spoon livers over salad and serve immediately.

Normandy mussels

9lb (4kg) mussels
1 onion
2oz (50g) butter
4 garlic cloves, crushed

1pt (600ml) dry cider
6tbsp chopped fresh parsley
1 French stick

Put mussels in cold water as soon as you get them home to prevent good ones from opening at this stage.

1 Put mussels in a sinkful of cold water. Discard any shells that are open. Pull fibrous part or 'beard' away from each shell, cutting away with a small sharp knife if stubborn. Scrub shells well with a nail brush and put into clean water. Leave until required.

2 Finely chop onion. Heat butter in a very large saucepan. Add onion and garlic and fry for 5 minutes until softened but not browned. Add cider and plenty of seasoning and bring to boil.

3 Drain mussels and add to pan, cover with a lid and cook for 6–8 minutes, until all shells have opened.

4 Sprinkle with parsley, ladle shells and cider mixture into large soup bowls. Discard any mussels with shells that have not opened and serve at once with thickly sliced French bread.

Shop around for mussels as prices vary widely; a fishmonger may charge less than supermarkets.

If you don't have a large enough saucepan, use two pans or use a preserving pan and cover with a baking sheet.

Gateau Paris-Brest with hot chocolate sauce

Measure choux pastry ingredients accurately, mixture should not be too runny.

When short of time, fill centre with whipped cream.

CHOUX PASTRY

little oil for greasing

2oz (50g) margarine

2½oz (65g) plain flour

2 eggs, size 3

½tsp vanilla essence

CHOCOLATE SAUCE

4oz (100g) deluxe cooking chocolate

2tbsp caster sugar

FILLING

2 egg yolks, size 3

2oz (50g) caster sugar

¾oz (20g) plain flour

¾oz (20g) cornflour

½pt (300ml) milk

2tsp instant coffee granules

TO DECORATE

icing sugar

1 Preheat oven to 425°F, 220°C, Gas 7. Lightly oil a baking sheet. To make choux pastry, put margarine in a saucepan with ¼pt (150ml) water, heat gently until margarine has melted then bring to the boil.

2 Take pan off the heat, sift in the 2½oz (65g) flour and beat well. Return to heat and stir until mixture forms a smooth ball that leaves the sides of the pan. Cool slightly.

3 Beat eggs and vanilla essence together then gradually beat into flour mixture, beating well after each addition until smooth and glossy.

4 Drop spoonfuls of mixture into a rough ring shape about 7in (18cm) in diameter. Cook for 25 minutes until well risen and browned.

5 Take out of oven, cut in half horizontally and put both halves on baking sheet so cut surfaces are uppermost. Return to oven for 5 minutes to dry. Leave to cool.

6 For filling, whisk together egg yolks and caster sugar in a bowl until thick and pale. Slowly whisk in sifted flour and cornflour.

7 Heat milk in a saucepan until just boiling then gradually whisk into yolks mixture until smooth. Pour milk mixture back into pan and bring to boil whisking until very thick and smooth. Whisk in coffee granules until dissolved. Cover surface with dampened greaseproof paper and leave to cool.

8 Put bottom half of choux ring on a serving plate. Spoon over coffee filling. Cover with second choux ring and dust with sifted icing sugar. Chill for at least 1 hour so pastry can soften slightly.

9 For chocolate sauce, break chocolate into pieces and put into a saucepan with sugar and 6tbsp water. Heat gently, stirring until chocolate has melted and sauce is smooth. Set aside.

10 Just before serving, warm sauce again and pour into a warmed serving jug (or microwave sauce briefly in its jug). Cut ring into portions and serve with sauce.

COUNTDOWN In the morning
Prepare and scrub mussels and leave in clean cold water. Make and fill Gateau Paris-Brest. Prepare chocolate sauce. Wash lettuce and keep in a plastic bag in the fridge. Assemble dressing ingredients.

30 minutes before serving
Toss salad in dressing and spoon on to plates. Cut up bread and put in a basket. Cook mussels, take off heat and keep hot. Cook starter and serve immediately. Warm chocolate sauce just before serving.

Chinese supper for six

MENU

Pancake rolls

Chicken stir-fry
Egg-fried rice
Sizzling steak with noodles

£ £

Toffee bananas

Don't make pancakes too thin or beansprouts will pierce the pancake when rolled.

Pancake rolls reheat successfully on a baking sheet at 400°F, 200°C, Gas 6 for 10 minutes.

If you don't have a frying pan the right size, substitute a larger one and make 6 pancakes.

Pancake rolls

PANCAKES

2oz (50g) cornflour

2oz (50g) plain flour

2tsp oil

3 eggs, size 3

FILLING

½ bunch spring onions, trimmed

½in (1cm) piece fresh root ginger, peeled

1tsp oil

1 garlic clove, crushed

6oz (150g) beansprouts, washed

½tsp sugar

1tbsp soy sauce

TO FINISH

oil for deep frying

1 Cut 12, 8in (20.5cm) squares of greaseproof paper.

2 To make pancakes, put cornflour, flour, oil, eggs and a pinch of salt into a bowl. Gradually whisk in ¾pt (450ml) water and mix until a smooth batter forms. Leave to stand for 15 minutes.

3 For filling, thinly slice spring onions, finely chop ginger. Heat oil in a frying pan or wok, add spring onions, ginger and garlic and fry for 1 minute. Add beansprouts and cook for 1 minute. Stir in sugar and soy sauce. Set aside.

4 Heat a little oil in a 7in (18cm) frying pan, drain off excess then add 3tbsp pancake mixture, tilt pan so mixture coats base evenly then cook for a couple of minutes until underside is pale golden.

5 Loosen pancake and slide out on to a piece of greaseproof paper. Do not cook second side.

6 Repeat process until about 2tbsp pancake mixture remains, stacking cooked pancakes between prepared sheets of greaseproof so they do not stick together.

7 Drain beansprout mixture well and divide between pancakes, cooked side upwards. Brush all round edges with a little raw pancake mixture, then fold in the sides. Roll up tightly.

8 Heat a saucepan half-filled with oil to 375°F, 190°C or until oil bubbles the moment a pancake roll is added. Cook rolls in batches until browned. Drain well on kitchen paper. Serve hot.

Suitable for a vegetarian.

Beansprouts are often sold in 12oz (325g) packets; the following recipe uses the remainder from this one.

Chicken stir-fry

2 chicken breasts	3tbsp yellow bean paste
½ bunch spring onions, trimmed	¼pt (150ml) chicken stock
2 carrots, peeled	1tsp cornflour
1tbsp oil	
6oz (150g) beansprouts, washed	

Substitute sherry for a couple of tablespoons of the stock if you have it.

Quick to make.

1 Cut chicken, spring onions and carrots into thin diagonal slices.

2 Heat oil in a wok or large frying pan, add chicken and stir fry for 5 minutes until browned.

3 Add spring onions and carrots and cook for 2 minutes.

4 Stir in beansprouts, yellow bean paste and stock. Mix cornflour to a smooth paste with a little water, add to pan and bring to boil, stirring until thickened. Serve immediately.

Egg-fried rice

A good recipe to use up leftover cooked rice. Vary the vegetables depending on what you have in the fridge, eg peas, pepper, celery, chopped beansprouts.

10oz (275g) long grain rice	1 egg, size 3
4oz (100g) button mushrooms, wiped	1 egg yolk, size 3
1 tbsp oil	2oz (50g) frozen peas, thawed

1 Cook rice in a large saucepan of boiling salted water for 8–10 minutes until rice is tender. Drain into a colander and dry pan.

2 Slice mushrooms. Heat oil in pan and fry mushrooms for 3 minutes.

3 Beat eggs and egg yolk with 2tsp water and seasoning, add to pan with rice and peas and cook for 3 minutes, stirring continuously, until eggs are scrambled. Spoon into a serving dish.

Use two whole eggs if not making Toffee bananas.

Quick to make.

Look out for frying steak in the supermarket as it is very much cheaper than rump steak and in this recipe no one will know the difference.

Sizzling steak with noodles

8oz (225g) broccoli	1 tbsp oil
10oz (275g) frying or rump steak	4tbsp Chinese barbecue sauce (hoisin sauce)
1 red pepper	
2 sheets dried egg noodles from an 8.8oz (250g) packet	

1 Cut broccoli into small florets and stems into strips. Cook in a wok or saucepan half-filled with boiling water for 3 minutes. Drain, rinse with cold water and drain again.

2 Trim any fat away from beef then cut diagonally into thin strips. Cut core and seeds from pepper and cut into thin strips.

3 Put noodles in a shallow dish, cover with boiling water and leave to stand for 6 minutes. Drain.

4 Heat oil in a frying pan, add beef and stir fry over a high heat for 2 minutes until browned. Add broccoli and red pepper and stir fry for 2 minutes.

5 Stir in hoisin sauce and 6tbsp water. Drain noodles and add to pan. Toss in the sauce and cook for 2 minutes until piping hot. Spoon into a serving dish.

Use remaining hoisin sauce for other recipes: brushing over grilled chops or spicing up meat or sausage casseroles.

Quick to make.

Toffee bananas

2tbsp sesame seeds	I egg, size 3
I egg white, size 3	5 bananas
2oz (50g) plain flour	oil for deep frying
2fl oz (60ml) milk	4oz (100g) granulated sugar

Best made at the last minute so get all the ingredients together before you sit down to eat, then cook once main course is eaten.

I Put sesame seeds into a nonstick frying pan or saucepan and heat gently, stirring constantly until lightly browned. Set aside.

2 Whisk egg white in a small bowl until soft peaks form. Put flour, milk and whole egg together in a second bowl, whisk until smooth then fold in the whisked egg white.

3 Thickly slice bananas. Reheat pan of oil used for pancake rolls to 375°F, 190°C or until a cube of bread rises and sizzles in 30 seconds. Dip bananas a few at a time into batter then into oil. Cook until golden brown. Drain on kitchen paper. Continue until all bananas are cooked.

4 While bananas are frying, add sugar and 2tbsp water to sesame seeds to make syrup. Heat without stirring until sugar has dissolved then boil rapidly until mixture turns golden brown.

5 Quickly put base of pan into a sink of cold water to stop syrup cooking further.

6 Brush a sheet of foil with a little oil, put bananas on top then drizzle sesame syrup over. Leave to cool for 2 minutes then peel off foil, put on plates and serve immediately.

COUNTDOWN **In the morning**

Make and fry pancake rolls, put on to a baking sheet and cover with greaseproof paper. Chill. Prepare ingredients for chicken stir fry and sizzling beef and put on 2 separate plates, cover with cling film and chill. Cook rice, cover and chill.

30 minutes before serving

Reheat pancake rolls in the oven. Make sizzling steak. Finish fried rice. Cook stir-fry chicken.

Make and cook toffee bananas after main course.

Curry supper for four

M E N U   *Spicy beef samosas with mint and apple raita*

Spinach dhansak

£   *Kulfi*

Spicy beef samosas

FILLING

1 onion, peeled

2 garlic cloves, peeled

1 dried red chilli

1 tbsp oil

1 tsp coriander seeds, coarsely crushed

1 tsp cumin seeds, coarsely crushed

½ tsp ground cinnamon

½ tsp ground turmeric

3 cloves

1 bay leaf

8oz (225g) minced beef

¼ pt (150ml) beef stock

PASTRY

8oz (225g) plain flour

8tsp sunflower oil, plus extra for deep frying

½ round lettuce to garnish

Freeze any leftover samosas when completely cold in a plastic bag for up to 6 weeks. Defrost for 4 hours at room temperature. Reheat on a baking sheet in a preheated oven at 400°F, 200°C, Gas 6 for 10 minutes.

If you want to prepare samosas in advance, put on to a sheet of greaseproof paper dusted with flour, cover with another sheet of greaseproof and chill until required. Cook just before serving.

1   Finely chop or process onion, garlic and chilli, including seeds.

2   Heat oil in a saucepan, add spices and bay leaf and cook for 1 minute. Add onion mixture and cook for 3 minutes, stirring until browned.

3   Add mince and fry, stirring, until evenly browned. Stir in stock and seasoning. Bring to the boil, cover and simmer for 45 minutes, stirring occasionally. Leave to cool.

4   To make pastry, put flour and a pinch of salt into a bowl. Add the oil and about 8tbsp water and mix to a firm dough. Knead on a lightly floured surface for 5 minutes until smooth.

For vegetarians, use a spicy potato and pea stuffing.

5 Divide into 12 equal pieces and roll each piece out on a floured surface to the size of a small saucer. Cut each in half. Brush the cut edge of each with a little oil.

6 Spoon a little meat mixture into the centre then fold tip of one cut edge up and over filling to give a triangle shape. Fold opposite tip across pastry so that filling is completely enclosed. Seal edges well.

7 Pour oil into a saucepan to give a depth of 2in (5cm). Heat oil to 375°F, 190°C or until oil bubbles immediately a samosa is added. Cook in batches for 3–4 minutes until browned.

8 Drain on kitchen paper. Finely shred lettuce and put on a serving plate, arrange samosas on top and serve with mint and apple raita.

Mint grows easily from seed – in a window box or in a pot on the windowsill as well as in the garden. A little mint jelly can be used instead.

Mint and apple raita

½oz (15g) fresh mint

1 red-skinned eating apple, quartered and cored

1 small green pepper, halved and deseeded

1 dried chilli, seeds removed

2tsp lemon juice

6oz (150g) natural yogurt

1 Finely chop or process mint, apple, green pepper and chilli.

2 Mix with lemon juice, yogurt and seasoning. Spoon into a serving dish.

Spinach dhansak

1 large onion, peeled

2in (5cm) piece fresh root ginger, peeled

2 garlic cloves, peeled

1 dried chilli

1 tbsp oil

1 tsp cumin seeds, coarsely crushed

1 tsp coriander seeds, coarsely crushed

1 tsp ground turmeric

8oz (225g) red lentils

1½pt (900ml) vegetable stock

1lb (450g) potatoes, peeled

8oz (225g) long grain rice

12oz (325g) frozen leaf spinach, just thawed

3 tomatoes

2oz (50g) creamed coconut

Use 1lb (450g) washed and shredded fresh spinach if preferred and cook until just wilted.

If creamed coconut is unavailable then infuse 4oz (100g) desiccated coconut in ½pt (300ml) boiling water. Strain and use liquid in place of ½pt (300ml) stock.

Suitable for a vegetarian.

1   Finely chop or process onion, ginger, garlic and chilli including seeds.

2   Heat oil in a large saucepan, add cumin, coriander and turmeric and cook for 1 minute. Add onion mixture and fry for 3 minutes, stirring until browned.

3   Stir in lentils, stock and seasoning. Bring to the boil. Cut potatoes into chunks, add to pan, cover and simmer for 25 minutes or until lentils are soft, stirring occasionally.

4   Bring a large saucepan of water to the boil, add rice and a pinch of salt. Bring water back to the boil and cook for 8–10 minutes until rice is just cooked.

5   Meanwhile, put spinach into a sieve and squeeze out excess liquid with the back of a spoon. Dice tomatoes and coconut.

6   Add spinach, tomatoes and coconut to lentil mixture, with a little extra water if needed. Cook for 3 minutes, stirring until piping hot. Drain rice, spoon on to serving plates and top with spinach mixture.

Use full-fat or semi-skimmed milk but not fat-free milk.

Make sure heat is only moderate or milk will burn on base of pan.

Beating the ice cream during freezing gives a better finished texture.

Uses store cupboard ingredients.

Kulfi

2pt (1.1 litres) milk

4 cardamom pods

3tbsp caster sugar

few pastel rose petals to decorate, optional

1 Put milk in a heavy-based pan and bring to the boil. Reduce heat and simmer for 1¼ hours, stirring occasionally, until reduced to about 1pt (600ml).

2 Crush cardamom pods with a pestle and mortar, picking out and discarding green pods. Strain milk into a plastic box and stir in cardamom seeds and sugar. Leave to cool completely.

3 Freeze for 4–5 hours until mushy then beat with a fork or put into a food processor. Return to plastic box and freeze until solid. Thaw at room temperature until just soft enough to beat. Beat thoroughly then return to freezer until solid.

4 To serve, soften at room temperature for 15 minutes. Scoop into glasses and sprinkle with rose petals, if liked.

COUNTDOWN **Day before**

Make kulfi and beat once.

In the morning

Beat kulfi, return to freezer. Make samosa filling and cool.

2 hours before serving

Make samosas and set aside. Make raita and prepare main course.

30 minutes before serving

Cook main course and rice. Deep fry samosas and drain well. Warm plates for main course and keep dhansak and rice hot while eating samosas. Take kulfi out of freezer just before eating main course. Scoop into glasses and decorate with rose petals just before serving.

Easy Italian supper for four

M E N U

Antipasto platter

Tagliatelle with spinach and mushrooms

£ £

Tiramisu

Prepacked salami is cut wafer thin — so you get 12 slices in a packet as opposed to only 8 or 9 to each 4oz (100g) when sliced at the delicatessen counter.

Quick to make.

Choose Italian salami, which is dark coloured and has a good flavour, not bright pink salami.

Antipasto platter

½ head celery

¼pt (150ml) mayonnaise

1tsp Dijon mustard

2½oz (65g) packet wafer-thin sliced Italian salami

2oz (50g) black olives

crusty bread to serve

1 Trim celery, reserving leaves for garnish. Wash stalks then thinly slice crossways.

2 Mix mayonnaise, mustard and seasoning together then stir in celery.

3 Arrange salami on plates and spoon on celery salad. Garnish with celery leaves and olives and serve with crusty bread.

Tagliatelle with spinach and mushrooms

12oz (325g) dried tagliatelle

8oz (225g) button mushrooms

7oz (200g) bag fresh spinach

2oz (50g) butter

2 garlic cloves, crushed

¼tsp grated nutmeg

¼pt (150ml) single cream

2oz (50g) fresh Parmesan, coarsely grated

1 Bring a large saucepan of salted water to the boil. Add pasta and cook for 8–10 minutes until just tender.

2 Meanwhile, rinse mushrooms and slice. Wash spinach thoroughly, drain, discard any stems and cut into thin shreds.

3 Drain pasta and dry pan, add butter and heat until melted. Fry mushrooms until golden then add spinach, garlic, nutmeg and seasoning. Toss together and cook for 2 minutes until spinach has just wilted.

4 Return pasta to pan, pour in cream and toss together until pasta is reheated. Spoon on to plates and sprinkle with Parmesan.

If using fresh pasta, add to boiling water, bring water back to the boil and cook for 2 minutes only.

Buying Parmesan cheese in a small block to grate freshly when needed is expensive but the taste transforms an otherwise inexpensive pasta dish. Keep remaining cheese in the fridge, well wrapped.

Quick to make, especially if you substitute fresh pasta.

For a strict vegetarian omit Parmesan and use vegetarian Cheddar.

Tiramisu

You can substitute mascarpone cheese; yogurt makes a cheaper alternative to the traditional recipe and is also lower in fat.

Cocoa can be used instead of drinking chocolate.

Quick to make.

3tsp instant coffee granules

6tbsp boiling water

6tbsp icing sugar

3tbsp sherry

1lb (450g) tub Greek-style natural yogurt

5oz (125g) sponge finger biscuits

1tsp drinking chocolate

1 Dissolve coffee in boiling water. Stir in half the sugar then add the sherry.

2 Stir remaining sugar into yogurt.

3 Dip biscuits one at a time into coffee mixture and arrange one third of them in the base of a glass serving dish. Spoon one third of the yogurt mixture over then repeat layers ending with yogurt.

4 Smooth surface and dust with sifted drinking chocolate. Chill until required.

COUNTDOWN One hour before serving

Make pudding and chill. Make starter and arrange on plates. Warm dishes for main course. Make main course and keep hot while eating starter.

Family Sunday lunch for six

M E N U   *Roast pork with mustard and honey crackling*
Apple and cumin stuffing
Apple sauce
Spicy roast potatoes and parsnips
Gingered carrots
Stir-fried cabbage

£ £   *Lemon meringue pie*

Roast pork with mustard and honey crackling

4–4¼lb (1.8–1.9kg) boneless
pork shoulder joint

little oil for brushing

2tsp Dijon mustard

1tbsp clear honey

2tbsp plain flour

1pt (600ml) vegetable or
chicken stock

1   Preheat oven to 400°F, 200°C, Gas 6. Score pork skin with a sharp knife if not already done. Brush with a little oil and sprinkle with salt. Put into a small roasting tin and cook in the centre of the oven for 30 minutes per 1lb (450g) plus 30 minutes.

2   Mix 1tsp mustard and the honey together and brush over pork skin 20 minutes before end of cooking.

3   To test: insert a skewer into thickest part of joint, juices will run clear when pork is cooked. Transfer joint to a serving plate and keep hot.

4   Drain fat out of roasting tin. Stir flour into meat juices. Gradually add stock and bring to the boil, stirring. Add remaining mustard, season and cook for 2–3 minutes. Strain into a gravy boat. Remove string from joint.

FOR GOOD CRACKLING

1 Make sure skin is dry before cooking, leave joint uncovered in fridge for several hours before cooking.

2 Score skin evenly and deeply, using a really sharp knife or a new blade on a Stanley knife.

3 Roast pork uncovered.

Buy bread when cheap and make the whole loaf into breadcrumbs using a liquidiser or food processor. Store in a plastic bag in the freezer. Use from frozen.

Apple and cumin stuffing

I onion, peeled

I cooking apple, peeled and cored

3tbsp oil

½tsp cumin seeds, roughly crushed

6oz (150g) breadcrumbs

I egg, size 3, beaten

1 Finely chop onion and apple and fry in 1tbsp oil until pale golden.

2 Take pan off heat and cool slightly. Stir in cumin, breadcrumbs, egg and seasoning and mix well.

3 Shape stuffing into small balls and set aside until ready to cook.

4 Add to pan of roast potatoes and parsnips, brush with 2tbsp oil and roast for 30 minutes until golden brown. Drain and arrange stuffing balls around roast pork.

Apple sauce

1 cooking apple, peeled, and cored

1tbsp caster sugar

4 cardamom pods

To microwave, put into a basin, cover with cling film, pierce and cook on Full Power (100 per cent) for 3 minutes. Leave to stand for 2–3 minutes then beat until pulpy.

1 Roughly chop apple and put into a saucepan with sugar and 1tbsp water. Crush cardamom pods with the flat of a knife and add both the pods and the seeds to apple.

2 Cover and simmer, stirring occasionally, until apples are pulpy. Remove pods leaving seeds, and spoon sauce into a serving dish. Serve warm or cold.

Spicy roast potatoes and parsnips

2lb (900g) potatoes, peeled

1½lb (675g) parsnips, peeled

5tbsp oil

1tsp ground turmeric

1tsp coriander seeds, roughly crushed

½tsp cumin seeds, roughly crushed

Crush seeds in a small bowl with the end of a rolling pin if you don't have a pestle and mortar.

1 Cut potatoes and parsnips into large chunks and cook in a saucepan of boiling salted water for 5 minutes. Drain.

2 Add oil to a large roasting tin and heat on shelf above pork for 5 minutes. Add spices then potatoes and parsnips and toss together.

3 Roast for 1¼ hours, turning once or twice, until golden. Drain and spoon into a warmed serving dish.

You will find root ginger in the fresh vegetables section in the supermarket. Store any leftover ginger with its skin on, in the salad compartment of the fridge for up to 3 weeks.

Quick to cook.

Gingered carrots

1 lb (450g) carrots, peeled

1 in (2.5cm) piece fresh root ginger, peeled

1 oz (25g) butter

1 Cut carrots into thin sticks. Finely chop ginger and set aside until required.

2 Cook carrots in a saucepan of salted water until just tender, about 10 minutes, depending on size. Drain and dry pan. Add ginger and butter and cook for 2 minutes.

3 Return carrots to pan with freshly ground black pepper, toss together then spoon into a warmed serving dish.

Cook cabbage at the last minute so it keeps its colour.

Stir-fried cabbage

1 lb (450g) green cabbage   1 tbsp oil

1 Finely shred cabbage discarding woody core. Set aside until required.

2 Heat oil in a wok or large frying pan, add cabbage and seasoning and stir fry for 4–5 minutes until cooked. Spoon into a warmed serving dish.

Lemon meringue pie

BISCUIT BASE	FILLING
2oz (50g) butter	1½oz (40g) cornflour
7oz (200g) digestive biscuits	4½oz (115g) caster sugar
1tbsp caster sugar	2 lemons, grated rind and juice
	3 eggs, size 3, separated

Don't make more than 2–3 hours in advance as meringue can separate. If you do want to prepare in advance, chill biscuit base and make lemon filling. Add topping and cook no more than 2 hours in advance.

1 Use a little of the butter to grease an 8in (20.5cm) ovenproof flan dish. To make biscuit base, put biscuits into a plastic bag and crush with a rolling pin until fine crumbs are formed.

2 Heat remaining butter in a saucepan until melted. Take off heat and stir in biscuit crumbs and sugar.

3 Spoon into dish and press over base and up sides with the end of the rolling pin. Chill for 30 minutes.

Spoon filling into a cooked pastry case if preferred.

4 Meanwhile, to make filling, mix cornflour, 1½oz (40g) sugar, lemon rind and 3tbsp water to a smooth paste in a saucepan. Make lemon juice up to ½pt (300ml) with water.

5 Whisk lemon juice and water mixture into cornflour mixture in pan then bring to the boil, whisking until very thick and clear. Cool slightly then whisk in egg yolks. Leave to cool completely.

6 Whisk egg whites in a clean, dry bowl until stiff. Gradually whisk in remaining sugar, 1tsp at a time and continue whisking until thick and glossy.

7 Spoon lemon mixture into dish, level surface then spoon on meringue. Swirl top with a spoon and cook at 400°F, 200°C, Gas 6 in the centre of the oven for 15 minutes until browned. Serve warm or cold.

COUNTDOWN FOR LUNCH AT 1PM

10am
Preheat oven to 400°F, 200°C, Gas 6. Prepare pork and put in the oven at 10.15am. Make biscuit base for pudding and lemon filling, chill.

10.45am
Prepare and parboil potatoes and parsnips. Prepare carrots and cabbage. Make stuffing balls and apple sauce.

11.30am
Heat oil in a roasting tin on shelf above pork, add spices and cook potatoes and parsnips. Make meringue and finish lemon meringue pie. Cook for 15 minutes on shelf beside pork, until browned.

12.15pm
Turn roast potatoes and parsnips, add stuffing balls and brush with oil.

12.45pm
Test pork and transfer to a serving plate. Warm dinner plates and vegetable dishes. Transfer potatoes to base of oven, or turn oven up if not quite browned. Make gravy. Cook carrots, stir fry cabbage.

1pm
Dish up.

Freeze-ahead dinner for six

M E N U   *Hot cheese soufflés*

Lamb and kidney bean pie with French beans
Duchesse potatoes

£ £   *Chocolate orange truffle cake*

Hot cheese soufflés

2½oz (65g) margarine

2oz (50g) plain flour

½pt (300ml) milk

3oz (75g) mature Cheddar cheese, grated

2tsp Dijon mustard

4 eggs, size 3

Fold egg whites carefully into cheese mixture so that you do not knock out all the air.

1   Melt the margarine in a saucepan, take off heat and use a little of the margarine to brush bases and sides of 6 individual ramekin dishes.

2   Return pan to heat and stir in flour, mix to a paste then gradually stir in milk and bring to the boil, stirring until thickened and smooth. Take off heat and stir in cheese, mustard and seasoning. Leave to cool.

To make soufflés ahead on the day, go up to step 3. Cover surface of mixture with cling film. Add egg yolks and whites just before baking.

3   Separate eggs and beat yolks into cooled cheese mixture. Whisk whites until softly peaking then beat 1tbsp into cheese mixture. Gently fold in remaining whites with a metal spoon then divide between ramekin dishes.

4   Open freeze until solid then cover top of each ramekin with cling film and put into a plastic box. Freeze for up to 3 months.

5   To serve, remove ramekins from freezer, unwrap and cut a strip of nonstick baking paper to go around each dish so that it stands 1in (2.5cm) above rim of dish.

Secure with paper clips or staple. Put on a baking tray. Defrost for 1 hour at room temperature.

6 Cook at 400°F, 200°C, Gas 6 on oven shelf above pie for 30 minutes until well risen and browned. Quickly remove paper and serve immediately.

Frozen lamb shoulder steaks are cheap; if unavailable in your local freezer centre use neck or stewing lamb instead and allow 12oz (325g) extra.

Check freezer shops for bargain priced wines and beers to serve with the meal.

For fan-assisted ovens cover pie loosely with foil after 20 minutes to prevent overbrowning.

Lamb and kidney bean pie

1tbsp oil

2¼lb (1kg) frozen lamb shoulder steaks, thawed

1 large onion, peeled

2tbsp plain flour

¾pt (450ml) lamb stock

14½oz (411g) can red kidney beans, drained

4 sprigs fresh rosemary or 1tsp dried

2tsp paprika

9oz (250g) frozen puff pastry, just thawed

4oz (100g) button mushrooms, wiped and sliced

TO SERVE

beaten egg to glaze

1lb (450g) frozen French beans

1 Preheat oven to 350°F, 180°C, Gas 4. Heat oil in a large frying pan, add lamb and fry over a high heat until well browned on both sides. Drain and transfer to a casserole dish.

2 Chop onion and add to pan, fry for 5 minutes until softened.

3 Stir in flour then add stock, beans, rosemary, paprika and seasoning. Bring to boil and pour over lamb. Cover and cook in oven for 1½ hours.

4 Roll out pastry on a floured surface until a little larger than pie dish. Place a 2pt (1.1 litre) shallow pie dish, rim side down, on pastry and cut around dish roughly.

5 Lift lamb out of sauce, take meat off any bone and cut into pieces. Put into the base of the pie dish. Add onion, beans, mushrooms and half the sauce.

6 Dampen edge of the dish and cut strips of pastry from trimmings. Press on to dish edge and brush with water.

7 Mark criss-cross lines on pastry and place over lamb. Press pastry edges together well and trim excess pastry. Make small horizontal cuts along edge of pastry with the edge of a knife and flute.

8 Open freeze overnight until solid. Wrap in cling film, label and freeze for up to 3 months. Freeze remaining sauce separately.

9 Defrost lamb and sauce overnight at room temperature then transfer to the fridge in the morning.

10 Preheat oven to 400°F, 200°C, Gas 6. Brush pastry with beaten egg, stand pie on a baking tray and cook on oven shelf just below centre for 35–40 minutes until pastry is well risen and browned.

11 Cook French beans in a saucepan of boiling salted water 5 minutes before serving. Reheat sauce.

Duchesse potatoes

1½lb (675g) potatoes, peeled

1 egg, size 3, beaten

2oz (50g) margarine

¼tsp grated nutmeg

beaten egg to glaze

Make sure potato is very smooth or piping tube will get blocked.

1 Cut potatoes into large chunks and cook in a pan of boiling salted water for 20 minutes until soft. Drain.

2 Mash potatoes with egg, margarine, nutmeg and seasoning until very smooth.

3 Spoon into a piping bag fitted with a large star tube and pipe 18 whirls on to a baking tray.

4 Open freeze overnight until solid. Lift off baking tray with a palette knife and pack into a plastic box. Seal, label and freeze for up to 3 months.

5 To serve, brush a baking sheet with a little oil, transfer potatoes to tray and defrost for 1 hour at room temperature. Brush with egg and cook above pie next to soufflés for 15–20 minutes.

Substitute 2tbsp Cointreau, Grand Marnier or brandy if liked for half the orange juice.

Buy supermarket own-brand deluxe cooking chocolate for good flavour and value.

Chocolate orange truffle cake

oil for greasing

2 eggs, size 3

2oz (50g) caster sugar

3tbsp plain flour

1tbsp cocoa powder

6oz (150g) deluxe cooking chocolate

½pt (300ml) whipping cream

1 large orange, grated rind and juice

TO DECORATE

1tbsp cocoa powder

1tbsp icing sugar

1 Preheat oven to 400°F, 200°C, Gas 6. Grease an 8in (20.5cm) springform tin and line base with greaseproof paper. Whisk eggs and sugar together in a bowl, ideally with an electric whisk, until very thick and whisk leaves a distinct 'trail' behind when lifted above mixture.

2 Sift in flour and cocoa and fold in gently. Pour into tin and cook for 15 minutes or until cake is well risen and top springs back when lightly pressed with fingertips. Cool in tin.

3 Take sponge out of tin and cut in half horizontally. Line base and sides of tin with 2 pieces of cling film then put one cake layer back into base of tin.

4 Break chocolate into pieces and melt in a bowl set over a pan of hot water. Meanwhile, whip cream until it just holds its shape.

5 Stir orange rind and 3tbsp juice into melted chocolate then fold into cream. Drizzle half the remaining orange juice over sponge in tin.

6 Pour cream mixture into tin, spread level then top with remaining sponge. Drizzle with remaining orange juice, wrap in cling film and freeze for up to 3 months.

7 To serve, defrost for 3 hours at room temperature. Remove tin and cling film and dust top with sifted cocoa.

8 To give a striped finish, cut 4 strips of greaseproof paper of differing widths and arrange criss-cross style over top of cake to leave strips of cocoa-dusted top showing. Sift icing sugar over these on top of cocoa then carefully remove paper revealing stripes. Transfer to a serving dish.

When melting chocolate, bring a pan of water to the boil then turn off. Put bowl with chocolate on top and leave to melt. Don't keep stirring or chocolate will lose its gloss.

COUNTDOWN **1 month in advance**
Make and freeze soufflés, pie, duchesse potatoes and truffle cake.

Night before
Defrost pie and sauce at room temperature. Transfer to fridge in the morning.

3 hours before serving
Take cake out of freezer.

1½ hours before serving
Take soufflés and duchesse potatoes out of freezer. Make paper collar to go around each soufflé. Decorate cake and put on to a serving dish.
Preheat oven to 400°F, 200°C, Gas 6.

40 minutes before serving
Brush pie with egg and cook pie on shelf just below centre of the oven. After 10 minutes cook soufflés on shelf above pie. 10 minutes later add potatoes to cook alongside soufflés. Warm plates. Put water on to boil for beans. Take soufflés out of oven, discard paper and serve immediately. Cook beans while clearing starter dishes.

Greek-style supper for four

MENU

Hummus

Stuffed cabbage leaves

£ £

Baklava

Quick to make.

Hummus is best made in advance so flavours can develop.

Use fresh or bottled lemon juice in this recipe.

Add tahini to taste if you have some — optional

Hummus

15.2oz (432g) can chickpeas

2 garlic cloves, crushed

3tbsp lemon juice

3tbsp oil

3tbsp milk

pinch paprika

TO SERVE

12 olives

½ cucumber

2 tomatoes

1 small onion

1tsp fresh mint leaves, chopped, or ¼tsp dried mint

2tbsp oil

1 packet pitta bread

1 Drain chickpeas and put into a food processor or liquidiser with garlic, lemon juice, oil, milk and plenty of seasoning. Mix to a smooth purée. Spoon into a serving dish. Sprinkle with paprika. Garnish with 2 of the olives to serve.

2 Dice cucumber, cut tomatoes into thin wedges and thinly slice onion. Put into a serving bowl with remaining olives, mint, oil and plenty of seasoning. Toss together and set aside.

3 Just before serving preheat grill. Sprinkle each pitta bread with a little water and grill for 2–3 minutes, turning once until hot and puffy. Cut into strips, wrap in a napkin to keep hot and serve in a small basket with hummus and salad.

Stuffed cabbage leaves

1 onion, peeled
1lb (450g) lean minced lamb
2 garlic cloves, crushed
½tsp ground cinnamon
pinch grated nutmeg

4oz (100g) green lentils
½pt (300ml) lamb stock
1lb 4oz (550g) jar passata
8 large green cabbage leaves

Cabbage leaves make a very good substitute for the traditional vine leaves

1 Finely chop onion and dry fry in a large saucepan with the mince, stirring until mince is evenly browned.

2 Add garlic, cinnamon, nutmeg, lentils and plenty of seasoning. Then stir in stock and ¼pt (150ml) passata. Bring to boil, cover and simmer for 1 hour, stirring occasionally, until lentils are soft. Cool.

Use hot serving plates or sauce will go cold quickly.

Serve with extra pitta breads if liked.

3 Meanwhile, trim away thick stem from back of cabbage leaves. Bring a large saucepan of water to the boil, add cabbage leaves, bring back to the boil and cook for 2 minutes.

4 Drain, rinse with cold water and drain again.

5 Lay cabbage leaves out on the work surface, trimmed side downwards and divide mince mixture between them. Fold left and right sides in then roll up to enclose filling. Place rolls close together in a shallow ovenproof dish with the join underneath. Cover with foil and set aside until needed.

Passata (made of sieved tomatoes) is sold in jars in most large supermarkets; if unavailable, use a carton of tomato juice.

6 Preheat oven to 400°F, 200°C, Gas 6 and cook covered cabbage parcels for 30 minutes.

7 Pour remaining passata into a saucepan, pour in any juices from cabbage parcels, season then reheat. Spoon a little sauce over the base of each serving plate and tilt to cover evenly. Place 2 cabbage parcels in the centre of each and serve immediately.

Melt butter in the microwave for 1 minute on Full Power (100 per cent).

Remaining filo pastry can be rewrapped and returned to freezer.

Nice served warm.

Add rose water to sugar syrup if liked.

Baklava

4oz (100g) walnut pieces

3oz (75g) caster sugar

1 tsp ground cinnamon

pinch grated nutmeg

2oz (50g) butter

½ × 14oz (400g) packet filo pastry, thawed if frozen

SYRUP

4oz (100g) caster sugar

1 lemon, grated rind and juice

1 Preheat oven to 375°F, 190°C, Gas 5. Finely chop walnuts and mix with sugar, cinnamon and nutmeg. Melt butter in a small saucepan.

2 Open out pastry and cut stack of pastry sheets into 3 even-sized rectangles 7 × 11in (18 × 28cm).

3 Arrange one of the rectangles of pastry sheets in a 7 × 11 × 1½in (18 × 28 × 4cm) tin; brush alternate layers of the pastry with melted butter.

4 Sprinkle half the nut mixture over surface then cover with second stack of pastry sheets, again brushing alternate layers of pastry with melted butter. Sprinkle on remaining nut mixture. Top with last rectangle of pastry, brushing with butter as before and brushing top surface with butter.

5 Mark top into 3 strips 11in (28cm) long then mark each into triangles. Cook for 30–35 minutes until pastry is golden.

6 For syrup, put sugar, lemon rind and juice and ¼pt (150ml) water in a small saucepan. Heat gently until sugar has dissolved then boil rapidly for 2 minutes. Pour over baklava and leave to cool.

7 Cut into triangles and arrange 2 or 3 on each serving plate.

COUNTDOWN **Day before**

Make and cook baklava and make hummus.

In the morning

Make salad. Make mince mixture and roll up in cabbage leaves when cool.

30 minutes before serving

Cook cabbage parcels. Grill pitta breads and serve with starter. Warm main course plates and baklava in oven while eating starter.

Saturday brunch for six

M E N U

Soufflé-stuffed tomatoes

Hash browns
Sausage wraps

£

Citrus salad

Make sure edges of
tomato are wiped dry
or filling won't rise.

Quick to make.

Soufflé-stuffed tomatoes

6 medium-sized tomatoes

I egg, size 3, separated

I oz (25g) Cheddar cheese, grated

½ tsp Dijon mustard

2 tsp fresh or frozen chopped chives or parsley

I Cut a slice off the top of each tomato then, using a
teaspoon, scoop out enough flesh to leave a firm shell.
Turn upside down to drain. Reserve tomato centres to
add to soups or casseroles.

2 Beat egg yolk, cheese, mustard and herbs together
in a bowl with a little seasoning.

3 Whisk egg white in a separate clean bowl until stiff.
Stir a little egg white into yolk mixture to slacken then
fold in remainder.

4 Spoon egg mixture into each tomato, wipe away any
spills and put tomatoes in a small roasting tin, adding 'lids'
to base of tin. Cook at 400° F, 200° C, Gas 6 on shelf above
sausages for 10–12 minutes until well risen. Serve at once.

Hash browns

1lb (450g) potatoes, peeled   2tbsp oil
1 small onion, peeled

1 Coarsely grate potatoes and pat dry with kitchen paper. Finely chop onion.

2 Heat 1tbsp oil in a large frying pan, add potato and onion, spread into an even layer and season. Cover and cook for 5 minutes on moderate heat until browned on the underside.

3 Loosen potato cake all around edges then cover pan with a plate, invert pan on to it and turn out. Heat remaining oil in the pan then slide potato cake back into pan with browned side uppermost.

4 Press flat with a wooden spoon, cover and fry for 5 minutes. Remove cover and fry for a further 2 minutes or until underside is browned and potatoes are cooked all the way through. Cut into wedges to serve.

Keep potatoes hot in the base of the oven still in pan if it has metal handles or slide back on to plate.

Quick to make.

Sausage wraps

6 large herby sausages   1 tsp Dijon mustard
6 rashers streaky bacon,   little oil for greasing
rind removed

1 Preheat oven to 400°F, 200°C, Gas 6. Prick sausages.

2 Run a round-ended knife along length of each bacon rasher to stretch until half as long again. Spread mustard on one side of each rasher.

3 Wrap bacon around sausages, mustard side down, and secure ends with halved wooden cocktail sticks. Lightly oil a roasting tin, add sausages and cook for 45 minutes, turning once until browned.

4 Remove cocktail sticks just before serving.

This recipe is also good barbecued or grilled.

Replace mustard with tomato relish or chutney if preferred.

Citrus salad

Markets often sell cut priced fruits at the end of the day. Citrus fruits keep in the bottom of the fridge for up to two weeks.

Quick to make.

Fat free.

2 grapefruit

1 ruby grapefruit

3 oranges

1 passion fruit

2tbsp clear honey

1 Cut peel and pith away from grapefruit and oranges with a serrated knife then cut fruit into segments. Arrange on six small serving plates.

2 Cut passion fruit in half and scoop out seeds with a teaspoon. Spoon over grapefruit and oranges then drizzle with honey. Chill until required.

COUNTDOWN 45 minutes before serving

Make citrus salad. Scoop out tomatoes and set aside. Warm plates. Prepare and cook sausages. Prepare and cook hash browns. Finish tomatoes and cook when sausages are browned and potatoes are nearly ready.

Slow-cook supper for six

M E N U   *Pork and chorizo hotpot*
with green peas

£   *Gourmet rice pudding*

Pork and chorizo hotpot

1 tbsp oil

6 medium-sized pork shoulder steaks

1 onion, peeled

3 carrots, peeled

2 sticks celery, trimmed and washed

2 tbsp plain flour

4 oz (100g) chorizo sausage

14 oz (397g) can tomatoes

½ pt (300ml) chicken stock

3 bay leaves

1¾ lb (800g) potatoes, scrubbed

½ oz (15g) margarine

TO SERVE

12 oz (325g) frozen peas

Choose shoulder steaks or spare rib chops depending on which is the better buy.

If you don't have a large shallow casserole dish then use a roasting tin — improve appearance of an old one by lining with foil.

Ideal for a slow cooker; follow manufacturer's manual for timings.

1 Preheat oven to 325°F, 160°C, Gas 3. Heat oil in a large frying pan and brown pork steaks on both sides. Drain and transfer pork to a large, shallow casserole dish.

2 Chop onion and carrots and slice celery. Add to pan and fry for 5 minutes until lightly browned. Stir in flour.

3 Thinly slice chorizo and break up tomatoes with a spoon, add to pan with stock, bay leaves and seasoning. Bring to boil then pour over pork.

4 Thinly slice potatoes and arrange overlapping over pork. Season and dot with margarine. Cook, uncovered on shelf slightly above centre of oven for 2½ hours.

A good recipe to make if you want to go out with friends and come back to a meal all ready and waiting.

Could substitute black pudding for chorizo; find either at the delicatessen counter.

5 Just before serving, cook peas in a saucepan of boiling salted water for 5 minutes. Drain and transfer to a warmed serving dish and dish up pork.

Could add a few roughly chopped dried apricots to soak with sultanas.

If you forget to soak fruit use 1 tbsp sherry and soak for 30 minutes while preparing main course.

Uses store cupboard ingredients.

Gourmet rice pudding

2oz (50g) sultanas
2tbsp sherry
3oz (75g) pudding rice
2oz (50g) caster sugar

1 ½pt (900ml) milk
pinch grated nutmeg
½oz (15g) margarine

1 Soak sultanas in sherry in a small bowl for 2 hours or overnight.

2 Put sultanas into a 2½pt (1.4 litre) ovenproof dish with rice and sugar.

3 Bring milk to the boil, pour into dish. Sprinkle with nutmeg and dot with margarine. Cook on shelf below pork for 2½ hours. Serve with cream if liked.

COUNTDOWN **Night before**
Soak sultanas in sherry.

3 hours before serving
Preheat oven to 325°F, 160°F, Gas 3. Make pork hotpot and put in the oven on shelf just above centre of oven. Make rice pudding and cook on lowest oven shelf. Cook peas 5 minutes before serving hotpot.

Speedy supper for six

M E N U   *Warm bacon and avocado salad*

Pesto and penne

£   *Cheat's yogurt brulée*

Warm bacon and avocado salad

5tbsp oil

1tbsp lemon juice or
wine vinegar

1 oak leaf or curly leafed
lettuce

6oz (150g) streaky bacon,
rind removed

3 slices bread

1 garlic clove, crushed

2 avocados

Cook this quick
starter just before
serving so bacon and
croutons are hot and
crisp.

Shop around for
avocados – they vary
greatly in price.

1   Make dressing by mixing 3tbsp oil, lemon juice or
vinegar and seasoning together in a large bowl.

2   Separate lettuce leaves, wash well, dry and then tear
into bite-sized pieces.

3   Chop bacon and dry fry in a nonstick frying pan until
crisp and golden. Drain and set aside on a plate; keep hot.

4   Dice bread. Add remaining 2tbsp oil to fat in bacon pan
then add bread and garlic and fry, stirring frequently,
until browned. Drain and put on bacon plate, keep hot.

5   Halve avocados, remove stones, peel and dice. Add
lettuce, avocado, bacon and croutons to dressing and toss
well. Spoon on to serving plates and serve while bacon is
still hot.

Pesto and penne

Don't buy expensive packets of fresh herbs — use whatever suitable herbs you have growing in the garden or omit altogether.

Substitute 3 tbsp grated Parmesan for Cheddar if preferred.

Uses store cupboard ingredients.

1 lb 2 oz (500g) dried pasta quills (penne)
2 onions, peeled
4 small dried chillies
4 tbsp oil
4 garlic cloves, crushed
2 × 14 oz (397g) cans tomatoes

1 tsp caster sugar
6 tsp pesto sauce
4 oz (100g) Cheddar cheese
sprigs of fresh oregano to garnish, optional

1 Bring a large saucepan of salted water to the boil. Add pasta, bring back to the boil and cook uncovered for 10–12 minutes until pasta is just tender.

2 Meanwhile, finely chop onions. Thinly slice chillies, do not discard seeds.

3 Heat oil in a separate saucepan, add onions and fry for 5 minutes, stirring occasionally, until golden. Add chillies, including seeds, and garlic and cook for 2 minutes.

4 Stir in tomatoes, sugar and plenty of salt and pepper. Bring to boil breaking tomatoes up with a spoon. Cover and simmer for 5 minutes, stirring occasionally until pulpy.

5 Drain pasta and add to tomato sauce with pesto sauce, mix well then spoon into bowls. Grate cheese and sprinkle over pasta. Garnish with sprigs of oregano if liked.

Cheat's yogurt brulée

little oil for greasing
6tsp demerara sugar
I kiwi fruit, peeled

2 ripe pears, peeled
I lb (450g) tub Greek-style natural yogurt

Vary the fruits depending on what is a good buy, such as a few strawberries or raspberries in season. If using grapes, take seeds out first.

I Line a baking sheet with foil, draw round the top of a ramekin dish and repeat to give 6 circles. Brush foil lightly with oil and sprinkle inside each circle evenly with demerara sugar.

2 Put the sugar circles under a hot grill until sugar has melted and caramelised. Cool.

3 Halve kiwi fruit and slice thinly. Quarter, core and slice pears. Divide fruit between bases of 6 ramekin dishes.

Sugar circles lose their crispness if added to brulées too far in advance.

4 Spoon yogurt over fruit and level surface. Chill until required.

5 Peel cooled caramel discs off foil and arrange on yogurt just before serving.

COUNTDOWN **I hour before serving**
Make brulées and put in the fridge. Leave sugar circles in the kitchen to cool and harden. Prepare tomato sauce for pasta. Grate cheese. Dice bacon and bread for salad. Wash lettuce and make dressing but do not mix together.

15 minutes before serving
Warm dishes for main course. Make pasta dish and keep hot in saucepan with lid on. Finish salad starter and dessert.

Quick meat-free supper for four

M E N U

£

Tomato tarts

Mediterranean vegetables with couscous

Minted strawberry and kiwi salad

Tomato tarts

For strict vegetarians, check that the puff pastry is made with vegetable fat.

1 tbsp oil	½ onion
9oz (250g) frozen puff pastry, just thawed	1 garlic clove, crushed
little plain flour for dusting	1 tsp pesto sauce
12oz (325g) tomatoes	8 pitted black olives

1 Preheat oven to 425°F, 220°C, Gas 7. Brush baking sheet with a little of the oil.

2 Roll out puff pastry thinly on a floured surface to a 10in (25.5cm) square, trim edges neatly then cut into quarters. Make small cuts along the edges of each with the back of a small knife then flute. Put on baking sheet, spaced slightly apart.

3 Thinly slice tomatoes and arrange overlapping on each pastry square. Season.

4 Finely chop onion and fry in remaining oil with garlic until softened but not browned. Stir in pesto and spoon over tomatoes. Add olives.

5 Cook for 15 minutes until pastry is well risen and browned. Transfer to serving plates and serve hot.

Mediterranean vegetables with couscous

I aubergine	3tbsp oil
9oz (250g) couscous	2 garlic cloves, crushed
I lemon, grated rind and juice	I tbsp plain flour
2 courgettes	½pt (300ml) vegetable stock
I red pepper	2tbsp frozen chopped parsley
I yellow pepper	

If you don't have a sieve large enough for cooking the couscous then line a colander or steamer with a new J-Cloth.

I Cut stalk off aubergine and slice thinly crossways. Cut any large slices in half then arrange slices on a tray and sprinkle with salt. Leave to stand for 20–30 minutes.

2 Meanwhile, put couscous in a bowl and cover with boiling water. Leave to stand for 5 minutes then fluff up with a fork, drain in a large sieve. Stir in lemon rind and seasoning.

3 Trim courgettes and cut into thin diagonal slices.

4 Halve peppers, cut away core and remove seeds. Cut into thin strips.

5 Rinse aubergine with cold water then wring out with hands to remove bitter juices.

6 Heat 2tbsp oil in a saucepan, add aubergine and fry over a high heat, stirring for 2 minutes until just browned. Add remaining vegetables and garlic and fry for 3 minutes until browned and softened.

7 Take off heat and stir in flour, then add stock, half lemon juice and seasoning. Set sieve of couscous over vegetables in pan, cover, return to heat and simmer for 10 minutes until piping hot.

8 Transfer couscous to a warmed serving dish, stir in remaining lemon juice and oil. Transfer vegetable mixture to a warmed serving dish and sprinkle with parsley.

Minted strawberry and kiwi salad

Make this when strawberries are at the height of the season and therefore cheapest.

1 lb (450g) strawberries, hulled

2 kiwi fruit, peeled

1 tbsp fresh chopped mint

1 tbsp caster sugar

Use fresh mint from the garden, or a pinch of dried mint instead.

1 Quarter strawberries, halve kiwi fruit lengthways and thinly slice. Put both into a serving bowl.

2 Sprinkle with mint and sugar, toss together and chill until required.

Quick to make.

COUNTDOWN **1 hour before serving**
Make fruit salad and chill. Slice aubergine and sprinkle with salt. Soak couscous in boiling water. Make tomato tarts and cook. Make main course while tarts are cooking. Warm plates. Keep tarts hot if still cooking main course. Turn off main course and serve starter.

Smart vegetarian dinner for four

M E N U   *Celery and Stilton soup*

Mushroom strudel with sherry sauce
Carrot purée
Nutty cauliflower and broccoli

Rhubarb sorbet

££

Celery and Stilton soup

I onion, peeled	2oz (50g) margarine
I medium-sized potato, peeled	I ½pt (900ml) vegetable stock
I head celery, stalks separated and washed	3oz (75g) Stilton cheese

1 Finely chop onion. Dice potato. Slice celery reserving leaves for garnish.

2 Heat margarine in a saucepan, add vegetables, stir until well coated then cover and fry gently for 10 minutes, stirring occasionally, until softened but not browned.

3 Stir in stock and seasoning. Bring to the boil then cover and simmer for 15 minutes. Cool slightly.

4 Dice Stilton discarding rind. Purée vegetable mixture in a liquidiser or processor with crumbled Stilton. Return to saucepan. Slowly bring to the boil, stirring occasionally, until cheese has melted.

5 Spoon into bowls and garnish with celery leaves.

If cooking for strict vegetarians, check the label on the cheese to make sure it isn't made with 'rennet' as this is an animal product. Vegetarian versions are available, ask counter staff if unsure.

Try to buy green celery so finished soup has a good colour.

Can substitute I lb (450g) leeks for celery.

Mushroom strudel with sherry sauce

If you have a microwave oven, remember you can melt margarine on Full Power (100 per cent) for 1 minute.

Substitute Madeira wine for the sherry if liked.

Buy mushrooms loose rather than boxed for a better price in the supermarket or look out for bargains in your local market. Choose field mushrooms with dark undersides for good flavour, if available.

I onion, peeled

3oz (75g) margarine

2tbsp sunflower seeds

1lb (450g) button mushrooms, washed

8oz (225g) small open-cup mushrooms, peeled

2 garlic cloves, crushed

¼tsp Chinese five-spice powder

3tsp soy sauce

3tbsp sherry

10oz (275g) packet frozen filo pastry, just thawed

2tsp cornflour

¼pt (150ml) vegetable stock

fresh herb sprigs to garnish, optional

1 Finely chop onion. Heat 1oz (25g) margarine in a large frying pan and gently fry onion and sunflower seeds until lightly browned.

2 Quarter button mushrooms and slice open-cup mushrooms. Add to onion with garlic and fry for 3 minutes, stirring, until just softened.

3 Stir in five-spice powder, soy sauce, sherry and seasoning. Cook 1 minute then tip mushrooms into a colander set over a bowl, drain well, reserving cooking juices.

4 Melt remaining margarine in a small saucepan. Lay a large piece of greaseproof paper on the work surface and place 2 sheets of filo pastry together to make one large sheet, overlapping about ½in (1.3cm) at join. Arrange so longest edges are horizontal to you.

5 Brush with a little margarine and place a third sheet of filo on top to cover centre join.

6 Place 3 more sheets of filo on top, this time with longest edges at right angles to you, brushing layers with more margarine.

7 Spoon mushroom mixture to make a heaped band along bottom third of pastry leaving a border of pastry at either end. Fold border over mushrooms then roll up like a Swiss roll beginning at base and using paper to help.

8 Brush a baking sheet with a little margarine and place pastry parcel on top with join underneath. Brush with remaining margarine and chill until required.

9 Preheat oven to 400°F, 200°C, Gas 6. Cook pastry parcel for 25–30 minutes, covering with foil if overbrowning towards end of cooking.

10 Meanwhile, mix cornflour to a smooth paste with a little of the reserved cooking juices in a saucepan. Stir in remainder of juices and add stock. Bring to the boil, stirring until thickened and smooth.

11 Cut mushroom strudel into thick slices and put on serving plates; pour a little sauce around and garnish with herbs if liked.

Carrot purée

1 lb (450g) carrots, peeled

1 Slice carrots and cook in a saucepan of boiling salted water for 25 minutes until soft.

Purée reheats well in the microwave.

2 Drain and purée in a liquidiser or processor with freshly ground black pepper. Spoon into a warmed serving dish.

If you don't have a liquidiser or processor then mash carrots instead.

Nutty cauliflower and broccoli

Substitute other types of nuts if you have them.

Steam vegetables over carrot pan.

½ cauliflower
8oz (225g) broccoli

1oz (25g) Brazil nuts
1oz (25g) margarine

1 Cut cauliflower into small florets and thickly slice a few of the leaves. Cut broccoli into small florets and slice stems lengthways.

2 Put into a steamer or colander set over a pan of boiling water, cover and steam for 10 minutes.

3 Meanwhile, roughly chop Brazil nuts. Heat margarine in a small frying pan or the dried carrot pan, add nuts and fry for 2 minutes.

4 Transfer cauliflower and broccoli to a warmed serving dish and pour nuts and margarine over.

Rhubarb sorbet

If buying fresh rhubarb sold with its leaves, trim and then weigh to ensure you have the correct quantity for the recipe.

Double or treble quantities if you have a glut of rhubarb in the garden.

6oz (150g) granulated sugar
12oz (325g) trimmed rhubarb
2 kiwi fruit

1 Stir sugar into ¾pt (450ml) water in a saucepan. Heat gently until sugar has dissolved completely then bring to the boil and boil rapidly for 3 minutes. Leave to cool then pour into a plastic box.

2 Slice rhubarb and put into saucepan with 2tbsp water. Cover and cook for 10 minutes, shaking pan occasionally until soft but still brightly coloured.

3 Cool slightly then purée in a liquidiser or processor. Pour into plastic box, stirring. Leave until completely cold then freeze overnight.

4 Take out of freezer and allow to soften for 20 minutes at room temperature. Beat in a liquidiser or processor until very smooth. Return to box and freeze until solid.

5 Peel and thinly slice kiwi fruit and arrange overlapping over the base of 4 serving plates. Put scoops of sorbet on top and serve immediately.

Forced rhubarb gives the best colour; you may need to add a few drops of red colouring if using older rhubarb.

COUNTDOWN

Day before (or complete recipe earlier if preferred)
Make sorbet.

In the morning
Beat sorbet and return to freezer. Make soup. Keep celery leaves in a bowl of cold water. Prepare strudel and chill until ready to cook. Make carrot purée. Cut cauliflower and broccoli into florets, set aside. Chop Brazil nuts and put into a saucepan with the margarine.

30 minutes before serving
Preheat oven. Take sorbet out of freezer and allow to soften for 20 minutes. Cook strudel. Put scoops of sorbet on to a baking sheet and put back into freezer. Reheat carrot purée either in an ovenproof serving dish covered with foil on shelf below strudel for 20 minutes, or, covered with pierced cling film in microwave on Full Power (100 per cent) for 3 minutes. Warm plates and serving dishes on base of oven.

10 minutes before serving
Steam cauliflower and broccoli. Finish sherry sauce. Reheat soup and serve.

Alfresco lunch for four

MENU   *Minted melon cocktail*

Mackerel and potato salad with horseradish dressing
Hot herb bread

£   *Peach and macaroon crush*

Minted melon cocktail

½ honeydew melon	1 tbsp fresh chopped mint
¼ cucumber	or ½ tsp dried
2 tomatoes	

Best to make a little in advance so minty flavour permeates melon, cucumber and tomato.

Garnish with sprigs of fresh mint if liked.

1 Scoop seeds out of melon with a spoon and cut away skin. Halve cucumber lengthways and scoop out seeds. Quarter tomatoes and scoop out seeds.

2 Dice melon, cucumber and tomatoes and put into a bowl with mint and seasoning. Toss together and chill until required.

Fat free and very low in calories.

3 Mix together and spoon into 4 small dishes.

Quick to make.

Mackerel and potato salad with horseradish dressing

12oz (325g) new potatoes, scrubbed

3 eggs, size 3

1 curly leafed lettuce

8oz (225g) smoked mackerel fillets

1 small onion, peeled

DRESSING

3tbsp mayonnaise

6oz (150g) tub natural yogurt

2tsp horseradish sauce

TO GARNISH

¼tsp paprika

Mayonnaise may be omitted for calorie-counters.

Quick to make.

1 Halve or quarter potatoes depending on size and cook in a saucepan of boiling salted water for about 10 minutes or until tender. Hard-boil eggs in a separate pan of boiling water.

2 Meanwhile, separate lettuce leaves, wash, drain and tear into bite-sized pieces. Arrange on a platter.

3 Peel skin off mackerel and break fish into large flakes. Thinly slice onion. Add to platter with fish.

4 Mix dressing ingredients together in a bowl.

5 Drain potatoes and eggs and cool under cold running water. Drain well. Peel and quarter eggs. Add to platter with potatoes and sprinkle with paprika. Serve dressing separately and spoon over just before eating.

Hot herb bread

4oz (100g) butter

3tbsp fresh chopped mixed herbs

1 French stick

Use white rolls for individual portions.

Substitute low-fat margarine for butter.

1 Preheat oven to 400°F, 200°C, Gas 6. Beat butter, herbs and a little pepper together.

2 Cut slits in bread then spread each side with butter. Wrap in foil and bake for 15 minutes. Serve hot.

Peach and macaroon crush

Single macaroons can be bought at a baker's shop or supermarket in-store bakeries.

Quick to make.

I large macaroon

7oz (200g) tub fromage frais

4 peaches

TO DECORATE

few mint sprigs, optional

1 Break macaroon into small pieces and stir into fromage frais.

2 Halve and stone peaches. Thinly slice and arrange on 4 serving plates like a fan. Divide fromage frais mixture between plates and decorate with sprigs of mint, if using.

COUNTDOWN **I hour before serving**

Make melon cocktail. Make mackerel and potato salad and dressing. Prepare herb bread and wrap in foil but do not cook. Make pudding and arrange on plates. Get everything together and put on trays ready to take outside to eat.

15 minutes before serving

Cook herb bread and leave in turned off oven while eating starter. Toss melon cocktail and spoon into dishes.

Picnic lunch for six

MENU

Raised pork pie

Carrot and sunflower seed salad

Potato salad

£

Chocolate brownies with fresh strawberries

Raised pork pie

FILLING

1½lb (675g) spare rib pork chops

1 onion, peeled

2 eating apples, peeled and cored

1 tbsp fresh chopped sage or 1 tsp dried

PASTRY

1lb (450g) plain flour

1 tsp salt

7oz (200g) lard

8fl oz (240ml) milk and water mixed

milk to glaze

Keep pastry for lid in a warm place as it becomes brittle and difficult to work when cold.

Brush pie with beaten egg if liked.

Can be frozen for up to 6 weeks, thaw overnight in a cool place.

1 Preheat oven to 350°F, 180°C, Gas 4. Cut any bones away from pork then coarsely mince, process or finely chop meat. Process or finely chop onion and apples.

2 Mix meat, onion, apples, sage and plenty of seasoning together in a bowl.

3 For the pastry, mix flour and salt together in a large bowl. Put lard and milk and water in a saucepan, heat until lard has melted then bring to the boil. Pour into flour and quickly mix to a smooth dough with a wooden spoon.

4 Reserve a quarter of dough for the pie lid and keep warm in bowl covered with a tea towel.

5 Pat remaining pastry into a circle the size of base of an 8in (20.5cm) springform tin. Lift into tin, press over base and work up sides of tin with fingertips until pastry overhangs top of tin slightly.

6 Spoon in pork filling, spread level. Roll out remaining pastry to the tin diameter. Dampen pastry edges in tin with milk. Add lid and press edges together well to seal. Trim and flute edges with finger and thumb.

7 Make a small steam hole in centre. Re-roll pastry trimmings, cut out leaves and arrange on top. Brush with a little milk and put pie on a baking sheet.

8 Cook for 1¾ hours. Loosen sides of pie with a knife, remove tin sides and cook pie for a further 15 minutes. Leave to cool then chill overnight in the fridge.

9 Remove tin base, pack into a plastic box for travelling and serve cut into thick slices.

Carrot and sunflower seed salad

Best made in advance so dressing flavour permeates the carrots.

Substitute sesame seeds or flaked almonds for sunflower seeds.

Uses store cupboard ingredients.

4tbsp oil	1lb (450g) carrots, peeled
4tsp vinegar	3tbsp sultanas
2tsp Dijon mustard	4tbsp sunflower seeds

1 Mix oil, vinegar, mustard and plenty of seasoning together in a plastic box.

2 Coarsely grate carrots and add to box with sultanas.

3 Dry fry sunflower seeds in a nonstick pan until lightly browned. Add to salad and toss together. Seal box well for travelling.

Potato salad

1½lb (675g) potatoes, peeled

½ bunch spring onions, trimmed

8tbsp mayonnaise

2tsp caraway seeds

Could substitute half the mayonnaise for natural yogurt.

1 Halve potatoes and cook in a saucepan of boiling salted water for 15–20 minutes until just tender. Drain, rinse with cold water and drain again.

2 Finely chop spring onions and put into a plastic box with mayonnaise, caraway seeds and plenty of seasoning.

3 Dice potatoes, add to mayonnaise and toss together. Seal box well for travelling.

Freeze plastic ice packs the night before. Add to cool bag when packing picnic so salad keeps fresh.

Chocolate brownies

4oz (100g) deluxe cooking chocolate

4fl oz (120ml) oil

8oz (225g) soft light brown sugar

2 eggs, size 3

3oz (75g) plain flour

1tsp baking powder

¼tsp salt

TO SERVE

1lb (450g) strawberries

Brownies may be baked at same time as pie on the shelf below.

1 Preheat oven to 350°F, 180°C, Gas 4. Line base and sides of a 7 × 11 × 1½in (18 × 28 × 4cm) tin with nonstick baking paper, snipping paper and folding into corners.

2 Break chocolate into pieces and melt in a bowl over a saucepan of hot water.

3 Beat oil, sugar and eggs together in a bowl or processor. Mix flour, baking powder and salt together. Add to oil mixture with melted chocolate and mix until smooth.

4 Pour into tin, ease mixture into corners and cook for 25–30 minutes until well risen and top is crusty.

Add 2oz (50g) walnut pieces or 4oz (100g) sugar-rolled chopped dates or both if liked at end of step 3. Brownies store well for up to 1 week in a plastic box or freeze for up to 3 months.

Look out for bargain-priced strawberries at your local market.

5 Cut into 12 bars and leave to cool in tin. Take out of tin and discard paper; pack brownies in a plastic box. Seal well. Wash strawberries, dry well and pack into a separate plastic box or bag and seal well.

COUNTDOWN   Night before

Make pie and brownies. Refrigerate pie when cool enough. Freeze plastic ice packs. Assemble picnic equipment.

In the morning

Make carrot and potato salads. Wash strawberries. Pack picnic bag.

Summer barbecue party for six

MENU   *Southern-style chicken*
Chicken parcels
Tossed green salad
Herby new potatoes

££   *Caramelised fruit salad*

Southern-style chicken

6 frozen chicken drumsticks, just thawed

2tbsp marmalade

2tbsp oil

2tbsp wine vinegar

2tsp paprika

1tsp mustard powder or Dijon mustard

1 Put chicken in a shallow dish. Mix remaining ingredients together, brush over chicken and leave to marinate for 1–2 hours.

2 Cook on a hot barbecue for 18–20 minutes, turning several times, until thoroughly cooked. To test, insert a sharp knife into meatiest part of one of the drumsticks; juices should run clear and meat should be an even colour. Serve hot with salad.

Make sure barbecue is on a level surface so it is stable while cooking.

Cooking should not start until coals have turned white – allow about 20 minutes for charcoal to heat up.

Keep a water sprayer handy to quench any flames when chicken juices fall on to charcoal.

Chicken parcels

Add sprigs of rosemary to barbecue coals when cooking for a lovely aroma and flavour.

If chicken appears to be cooking too quickly move slightly away from centre of coals or raise the grill rack up a little.

If any chicken parcel shows pink when cut open, microwave one at a time for 2 minutes and retest.

If stuffing ends become overbrown, trim away just before serving.

6 frozen chicken thighs, just thawed	1 egg yolk, size 3
1 small onion, peeled	1 tsp chopped fresh rosemary or ¼tsp dried
4oz (100g) button mushrooms	6 rashers smoked back bacon, rind removed
1 tbsp oil	fresh rosemary to garnish, optional
2oz (50g) fresh breadcrumbs	

1 Remove skin from chicken with a sharp knife, turn over and cut away bone. Open out thighs and put on a plate.

2 Finely chop onion and mushrooms. Heat oil in a frying pan, add onion and mushrooms and fry for 5 minutes, stirring frequently.

3 Take pan off heat and stir in breadcrumbs, egg yolk and rosemary. Season and divide mixture between chicken thighs. Press stuffing flat then roll up each chicken thigh and wrap with bacon. Secure each with a cocktail stick. Set aside until required.

4 Cook on a preheated barbecue for 25 minutes, turning several times until thoroughly cooked. To test, insert a knife into meatiest part of one of the thighs; juices should run clear and meat should be an even colour. Garnish with rosemary if liked.

Tossed green salad

4½oz (115g) packet mixed salad leaves

1 small onion, peeled

4tbsp oil

1tbsp red or white wine vinegar

½tsp mustard powder or Dijon mustard

Dressing should not be added until ready to eat or salad will wilt.

1 Tear salad leaves into bite-sized pieces, peel and thinly slice onion; put both into a salad bowl.

2 Put remaining ingredients into a screw-top jar with plenty of seasoning, close tightly and shake to mix. Pour dressing over salad leaves and toss together just before serving.

You can substitute lemon juice for vinegar.

Keep any leftover dressing in the fridge for up to 2 weeks.

Quick to make.

Herby new potatoes

1½lb (675g) new potatoes, scrubbed

2oz (50g) butter

2tbsp fresh chopped chives

2tsp fresh chopped rosemary leaves or ½tsp dried

Vary the herbs depending on what is available in the garden.

1 Halve any large potatoes and cook in a saucepan of boiling salted water for 20 minutes until tender.

2 Drain potatoes and return to pan with butter, herbs and black pepper. Toss together until butter melts then spoon into a serving dish.

Snip herbs into pan with scissors for speed.

Quick to make.

Look out for bargain priced pineapples in your local market.

Add a dash of sherry or brandy to fruit at the end of cooking if the budget allows.

Substitute bananas for pineapple.

Caramelised fruit salad

I medium pineapple	I oz (25g) butter
2 oranges	2oz (50g) demerara sugar
I red-skinned eating apple	

I Cut green top off pineapple, halve fruit then cut into slices cutting away skin and core. Cut peel away from oranges then cut into segments. Quarter, core and slice apple.

2 Make a foil tray by folding up the edges of a large sheet of foil. Add fruit, dot with butter and sprinkle with sugar.

3 Place on hot barbecue and cook for 10 minutes, turning fruit several times until butter has melted and fruit caramelised.

COUNTDOWN

In the morning
Marinate chicken drumsticks. Prepare and stuff chicken thighs. Wash salad, make dressing but do not toss together. Scrub potatoes. Prepare pineapple and oranges, but not apples as they go brown. Shape foil tray for fruit.

I hour before serving
Set up barbecue.

45 minutes before serving
Light the barbecue and when coals are white hot start chicken parcels. 5 minutes later add drumsticks. Cook potatoes. Toss salad. Add apple to other fruits. Cook pudding after main course is served.

Store cupboard supper for four

M E N U   *French onion soup*

Potato gnocchi with tomato sauce

£   *Crème caramel*

French onion soup

1 ½lb (675g) onions, peeled

1oz (25g) margarine

1tbsp oil

2 garlic cloves, crushed

2tsp granulated sugar

2pt (1.1 litres) beef stock

TOPPING

1 small French stick

1 garlic clove

sprig of fresh thyme or ¼tsp dried

2oz (50g) Cheddar cheese, grated

If you don't have a French stick then use two rolls cut into thin slices, or a slice of bread, trimmed to size of bowl for each serving.

Slice onions in a food processor for speed.

For vegetarians, use vegetable stock.

1 Thinly slice onions. Heat margarine and oil in a large saucepan. Add onions, stir to coat in oil mixture then cover and fry gently for 10 minutes, stirring occasionally, until softened.

2 Add garlic and sugar, increase the heat and fry uncovered for 15 minutes, stirring more frequently as onions begin to brown. Fry until onions are deep brown.

3 Add stock and plenty of seasoning. Bring to boil, cover and cook for 15 minutes.

4 To make topping, slice bread thinly then toast lightly on both sides. Halve garlic clove and rub over one side of each slice of bread. Sprinkle with thyme leaves and grated cheese. Ladle soup into grill-proof bowls, float two bread 'croûtes' on each and cook under a hot grill until cheese has melted.

Potato gnocchi with tomato sauce

1 ½lb (675g) potatoes, peeled

1 egg, size 3

1 egg yolk, size 3

2oz (50g) Cheddar cheese, grated

2tbsp grated Parmesan

6oz (150g) self-raising flour

SAUCE

1 onion, peeled

2tbsp oil

2 garlic cloves, crushed

14oz (397g) can tomatoes

¼tsp sugar

2 sprigs fresh thyme or ¼tsp dried

TO FINISH

2oz (50g) margarine

sprig fresh thyme or pinch dried thyme

2tbsp grated Parmesan

Save egg whites from this and crème caramel and freeze in a plastic bag for up to 6 weeks. Defrost and use for plum and cinnamon meringue gateau, in the Harvest supper menu.

Substitute vegetarian Cheddar for Parmesan if cooking for a strict vegetarian.

Microwave margarine and thyme for 1 minute on Full Power (100 per cent).

If tomato sauce is too thick when reheating, add a little water.

1 Cut potatoes into chunks then cook in a saucepan of boiling salted water for 20 minutes until soft. Drain and mash well.

2 Beat whole egg and yolk together then stir into potatoes. Add Cheddar and Parmesan cheeses, flour and seasoning and mix well. Leave until cool enough to handle then shape into walnut-sized balls with floured hands.

3 Put on to a baking sheet lined with floured greaseproof paper and flatten each slightly with a fork. Cover with greaseproof paper and set aside until ready to cook.

4 To make sauce, chop onion and fry in oil for 5 minutes until softened. Add garlic, tomatoes, sugar, thyme and seasoning and cook for 5 minutes, breaking tomatoes up with a spoon until thick and pulpy.

5 Bring a large saucepan or deep frying pan of water to the boil. Add a few potato balls, bring water back to boil and cook for 5–6 minutes until all the balls have risen to the surface and have puffed up. Cook in 2–3 batches. To test, remove one with a draining spoon, cut open and taste; it should be light and just cooked through. If still raw-tasting, cook 1–2 minutes more.

6 Lift out of pan, drain in a colander then put into a hot serving dish. Melt margarine in a pan with thyme. Brush a little over gnocchi and keep hot in the oven while cooking remainder.

7 To serve, pour hot tomato sauce over gnocchi, sprinkle with Parmesan cheese and black pepper.

Crème caramel

CARAMEL
4oz (100g) caster sugar

CUSTARD
1pt (600ml) milk

2 eggs, size 3
2 egg yolks, size 3
2tbsp caster sugar

Don't be tempted to stir sugar syrup while cooking or it will crystallise.

1 Put a 2pt (1.1 litre) deep ovenproof dish in a roasting tin.

2 To make the caramel, put the sugar in a saucepan with 4tbsp water. Heat slowly without stirring until sugar has dissolved then boil rapidly for 4–5 minutes until syrup is just turning golden.

Be careful when adding boiling water to syrup as it can spit, and have cold water ready in the sink.

3 Add 1tbsp boiling water and quickly put pan base in cold water in sink bowl so syrup doesn't overcook. When bubbles have subsided pour into dish and tilt dish so caramel coats base and sides. Leave to cool.

4 Preheat oven to 350°F, 180°C, Gas 4.

Warm milk in the microwave if preferred for 3 minutes on Full Power (100 per cent).

5 Bring milk to the boil in a saucepan. Take off heat and whisk in whole eggs, egg yolks and sugar. Strain into dish. Cover with foil, half fill roasting tin with boiling water and bake for 50–60 minutes or until custard is set.

6 Take dish out of roasting tin. Leave to cool then transfer to fridge until required.

7 Loosen all round edge of custard with a knife, then dip base of dish in hot water for 20 seconds to melt caramel. Turn out on to a plate and serve immediately.

COUNTDOWN   In the morning

Make crème caramel. Make and shape gnocchi. Make tomato sauce. Make onion soup. Toast croûtes, put them on to a baking sheet and cover with cling film.

20 minutes before serving

Cook gnocchi. Reheat onion soup. Warm main course plates. Ladle soup into bowls, add croutes and grill. Keep gnocchi hot in oven and start reheating tomato sauce while eating soup. Add tomato sauce and Parmesan just before serving gnocchi. Turn out crème caramel when ready to eat.

Harvest supper for six

M E N U   *Chunky tomato soup with pesto croutons*

Lemony roast chicken
Roast potatoes with thyme
Glazed carrots and turnips
French-style peas

£ £   *Plum and cinnamon meringue gateau*

Chunky tomato soup with pesto croutons

2 onions, peeled

1 medium-sized potato, peeled

2tbsp oil

1 ½lb (675g) tomatoes

2 garlic cloves, crushed

1tbsp plain flour

1 ½pt (900ml) chicken stock

1 tsp caster sugar

3tsp pesto sauce

CROUTONS

4 thick slices bread

2oz (50g) margarine

1 tsp pesto sauce

To freeze: pack cooled soup into a plastic box, freeze bread without topping in a plastic bag for up to 3 months.

Suitable for a vegetarian if vegetable stock is used.

1   Finely chop onions and potato. Heat oil in a large saucepan, add onions and potato, cover and fry for 10 minutes, stirring occasionally, until golden.

2   Meanwhile, remove any green tops from tomatoes and cut a cross in each base. Put into a bowl, cover with boiling water and leave for 30 seconds until skins loosen and burst.

3   Drain tomatoes, peel away skin and roughly chop. Add to onion mixture with garlic and cook for 3 minutes. Stir in flour then add stock, sugar and plenty of salt and pepper.

Home-made stock and well flavoured tomatoes make all the difference to this recipe. Avoid varieties of salad tomato which look perfect but lack taste.

4 Bring to boil, stirring, then half cover and simmer for 25 minutes. Stir in the 3tsp pesto.

5 For croutons, cut bread into diamond shapes and put on to a baking sheet. Beat margarine and pesto together then spread over one side of each bread shape.

6 Cook under a hot grill for 2 minutes until lightly browned. Turn croutons over, spread with remaining pesto mixture and grill as before.

7 Ladle soup into bowls and serve with hot croutons.

Lemony roast chicken

Make sure chicken is thoroughly defrosted before cooking. Never try to thaw by putting in warm water; this can be a health hazard. Microwave on defrost setting (30 per cent) or put in cold water and change several times.

Garnish with fresh thyme if available, putting a bunch at leg end to conceal joints.

I medium-sized leek, trimmed

I lemon, grated rind and juice

I tsp fresh thyme leaves or ½tsp dried

8oz (225g) full-fat cream cheese

3½lb (1.6kg) chicken, thawed if frozen

I tbsp oil

2tbsp plain flour

¾pt (450ml) vegetable or chicken stock

1 Preheat oven to 400°F, 200°C, Gas 6. Chop leek finely and wash thoroughly, drain well and put in a bowl with lemon rind, 1tbsp juice, thyme, cream cheese and seasoning. Beat together until smooth.

2 Remove trussing string from chicken and wash inside well with cold water. Drain.

3 Put chicken on a chopping board and loosen skin at top of breast bone with a small knife. Slide finger under skin and ease skin away from meat over chicken breasts and top of legs. The skin is quite strong, but be careful not to slit it.

4 Spoon teaspoonfuls of cream cheese mixture into space created under skin. Spread out evenly by pressing chicken skin from the outside. Tie chicken into a good shape with trussing string.

5 Put in a roasting tin and brush with oil. Cover loosely with foil and roast on shelf just below centre of oven for 1¼ hours. Remove foil, spoon juices over chicken and cook uncovered for 45 minutes until browned.

6 To test, insert a skewer into thickest part of leg, juices will run clear when thoroughly cooked. Transfer to a serving plate and keep hot.

7 Drain off all but 3tbsp of meat juices from roasting tin. Stir in flour then add remaining lemon juice, stock and seasoning. Bring to the boil, stirring. Strain into a gravy boat.

Roast potatoes with thyme

3lb (1.4kg) potatoes, peeled

3tbsp oil

2tsp fresh thyme leaves or 1tsp dried

3tsp rock salt

1 Cut potatoes into chunks and put in a saucepan of cold salted water. Bring to the boil and cook for 5 minutes.

2 Add oil to a large roasting tin and heat on shelf above chicken for 5 minutes. Add thyme, potatoes and salt and toss together.

3 Roast for 1¼ hours, turning once or twice until golden. Spoon into a warmed serving dish.

For a crisp finish, shake parboiled potatoes in colander until surfaces are roughened all over before roasting.

Transfer potatoes to base of oven and keep hot until chicken is ready.

Add 2tsp sesame seeds to the demerara sugar if liked.

Can use butter, as the flavour is better.

Glazed carrots and turnips

1lb (450g) carrots, peeled   1oz (25g) margarine
1lb (450g) turnips, peeled   1tbsp demerara sugar

1 Halve carrots lengthways and cut into thick slices. Cut turnips into wedges. Cook in a saucepan of boiling salted water for 15 minutes or until tender. Drain in a colander.

2 Dry pan. Melt margarine, return carrots and turnips to pan with sugar and seasoning. Cook over a high heat for 5 minutes, stirring frequently, until browned. Spoon into a serving dish.

Quick to make.

Serve this immediately so that lettuce is hot but still bright green.
Can use butter instead of margarine.

French-style peas

12oz (325g) frozen peas
1 round lettuce
1oz (25g) margarine

1 Cook peas in a saucepan of boiling salted water for 5 minutes.

2 Meanwhile, separate lettuce leaves, wash, drain and roughly shred.

3 Drain peas into a colander. Dry pan, add margarine and melt. Return peas to pan, add lettuce and cook very briefly, stirring until lettuce has just wilted. Spoon into a serving dish and serve immediately.

Peas are cheapest bought in very large bags: weigh out the quantity needed.

Plum and cinnamon meringue gateau

3 egg whites, size 3

6oz (150g) caster sugar

½tsp ground cinnamon

FILLING

1lb (450g) plums

2oz (50g) caster sugar

¾tsp ground cinnamon

7oz (200g) Greek-style natural yogurt

Use dried egg white if preferred; reconstitute according to packet directions.

1 Preheat oven to 225°F, 110°C, Gas ¼. Line a large baking sheet with nonstick baking paper and draw on two 8in (20.5cm) circles using a plate as a guide.

2 Whisk egg whites in a large clean bowl until stiff. Mix sugar and ½tsp cinnamon together then gradually whisk into egg whites, 1tsp at a time and continue whisking for a minute or two until mixture is thick and glossy.

3 Divide mixture between drawn circles and spread roughly with the back of the spoon. Cook for 1¼–2 hours or until meringues may be peeled easily off paper. Leave to cool.

4 Meanwhile, halve plums and put into a saucepan with the sugar, ½tsp cinnamon and 4tbsp water. Cover and simmer for 5 minutes until plums are just cooked.

5 Drain plums reserving juice. Discard stones, leave plums to cool.

6 To finish, put one meringue round on to a serving dish. Reserve about 2tbsp yogurt and choose 6 neat plum halves for topping; set aside. Spread remaining yogurt over meringue, arrange plums on top then cover with second meringue.

7 Just before serving arrange reserved plums and teaspoonfuls of yogurt alternating in a decorative border around top, dust with remaining cinnamon.

If any egg yolk gets into the bowl of egg whites scoop it out carefully with a piece of egg shell – even the smallest amount of yolk will prevent whites from whisking well.

Add topping just before serving or juice from plums may spoil appearance of meringue.

COUNTDOWN

The day before

Make and cook the meringue.

In the morning

Make or thaw the soup, cut croutons, cover with cling film on a baking sheet; do not cook. Make pesto mixture. Prepare chicken, spoon cream cheese under skin, put on a plate, wrap loosely in foil and chill. Peel potatoes and leave in a bowl covered with cold water. Peel carrots and turnips and put in a plastic bag in the fridge. Cook plums and leave to cool.

For dinner at 7.30pm

Preheat oven at 5.15pm. Roast chicken. Parboil potatoes and roast on shelf above chicken 30 minutes after it went into oven.

6.45pm

Sandwich meringues with yogurt and plums.

7pm

Warm plates. Cook carrots and turnips. Drain and cook in butter and sugar. Test chicken and transfer to serving plate, spoon potatoes around and return to turned-off oven. Make gravy. Cook peas. Reheat soup, grill croutons and serve. Add lettuce to peas just before serving. Decorate top of meringue just before serving.

'Best of British' supper for six

M E N U   *Cockles in parsley sauce*

Bangers and mash with beery onion gravy

£   *Sultana syrup sponge*

Cockles in parsley sauce

8oz (225g) shelled cockles, defrosted if frozen

3 rashers streaky bacon, rind removed

1½oz (40g) margarine

1½oz (40g) plain flour

¾pt (450ml) milk

3tbsp chopped fresh or frozen parsley

1oz (25g) Cheddar cheese, grated

1tbsp fresh breadcrumbs

If you do not have any ramekin dishes ask the fishmonger if he has any spare scallop shells. Scrub well before using.

1   Put cockles in a colander and wash well with cold water. Drain thoroughly.

2   Grill bacon until browned then finely chop.

Wash cockles well or any sand still on them will make the dish taste 'gritty'.

3   Melt margarine in a saucepan, stir in flour and cook for 1 minute. Gradually stir in milk and bring to the boil, stirring, until thickened and smooth.

4   Season well and stir in cockles, bacon and parsley. Divide between 6 ramekin dishes and sprinkle with cheese and breadcrumbs. Put on a baking sheet.

5   Cook under a preheated grill for 4–5 minutes until browned and piping hot.

If making earlier in the day make sure sauce is cool before adding cockles. Store in fridge until needed.

Can substitute English mustard but use less, as it may be stronger.

If you don't have a steamer then set a colander over potato pan and cover with a lid from a large saucepan.

Fry onions until well browned so gravy is full of flavour.

Bangers and mash with beery onion gravy

1lb (450g) potatoes, peeled
1lb (450g) swede, peeled
1lb (450g) green cabbage
1½lb (675g) pork sausages
1 large onion, peeled
2tbsp oil
3tbsp plain flour

¾pt (440ml) can best bitter
¼pt (150ml) beef stock
2tsp coarse grain mustard
1oz (25g) margarine
2tbsp milk

1 Cut potatoes and swede into chunks and cook in a saucepan of boiling salted water for 20 minutes until tender.

2 Finely shred cabbage, discarding core, season and cook in a steamer over potatoes for last 10 minutes of cooking, stirring once.

3 Meanwhile, prick and grill sausages for 15 minutes, turning several times until evenly browned.

4 Halve and thinly slice onion. Heat oil in a saucepan, add onion and fry for 10 minutes until softened and browned.

5 Stir in flour then add beer, stock, mustard and seasoning. Bring to boil, stirring, and simmer for 5 minutes.

6 Drain and mash potatoes and swede with margarine, milk and pepper. Spoon into a serving dish. Spoon sausages on to serving plate. Spoon cabbage into a dish. Keep hot while eating starter. Reheat gravy and pour into a gravy boat just before serving.

Sultana syrup sponge

little oil for greasing

8oz (225g) golden syrup

6oz (150g) plain flour

1 tsp bicarbonate of soda

1 tsp ground cinnamon

4oz (100g) fresh white breadcrumbs

5oz (125g) shredded suet

1 egg, size 3, beaten

1 orange, grated rind and juice

4fl oz (120ml) milk

6oz (150g) sultanas

TO SERVE

extra golden syrup

¼pt (150ml) single cream, optional

A 2½pt (1.4 litre) pudding basin has a 7in (18cm) diameter top.

When tying foil in place add a string handle so you don't burn your fingers when lifting basin out of pan.

1 Brush a 2½pt (1.4 litre) pudding basin with a little oil and line base with a circle of greaseproof paper. Add 3tbsp golden syrup. Put remainder into a large bowl.

2 Sift flour, bicarbonate and cinnamon into bowl. Add remaining ingredients, except serving ones, and mix well.

Turn pudding off when ready and leave in saucepan to keep warm.

3 Spoon mixture into pudding basin and level top. Cover with a pleated piece of double thickness greaseproof paper and foil. Tie securely around basin with string.

4 To cook, stand pudding on an upturned saucer in a large saucepan, half filled with hot water, or place in a steamer over a pan of hot water. Cover and steam for 2 hours. Top up water several times during cooking to prevent it boiling dry.

Uses store cupboard ingredients.

5 Remove foil, paper and string. Press centre of pudding with fingertips: if cooked, pudding will spring back, if not re-cover and cook for 20 minutes more. Loosen edge of pudding and turn out on to a plate. Serve with extra syrup and cream if liked.

COUNTDOWN **2½ hours before serving**

Make pudding and put on to steam. Make starter and set aside.
Prepare vegetables. Make gravy.

30 minutes before serving

Warm serving dishes. Put potato and swede on to cook.
Cook sausages then steam cabbage. Reheat gravy. Mash potato
and swede. Put vegetables into serving dishes and keep hot
in the oven. Grill starter and serve. Turn out pudding just
before serving.

Bonfire night party for eight

M E N U   *Mulled wine*

Chillied bangers and beans
Jacket potatoes with yogurt or spiced butter

£££   *Caramelised apple tart*

Mulled wine

1.5 litre bottle red wine	1 tsp whole cloves
1pt (600ml) orange juice	4oz (100g) caster sugar
2 cinnamon sticks, halved	1 orange

1 Put all ingredients except whole orange into a large saucepan. Add ½pt (300ml) water and bring slowly just to the boil, stirring occasionally.

2 Remove from heat and set aside for 30 minutes so flavours can develop.

3 Slice orange thinly, crossways, without peeling, add to pan and reheat wine. Ladle into heatproof glasses.

Quick to make.

Shop around for cheap wine — Bulgarian red wine is often inexpensive.

Do not boil wine or the taste will be spoilt.

If you have a slow cooker, use it to keep wine hot.

Chillied bangers and beans

Buy sausages from the delicatessen counter in the supermarket — much cheaper than buying prepacked. You should get 16 sausages for 2lb (900g); ensure you ask for two per person.

Keep a few sausages back to grill and serve plain if young children are in the party.

If you like your chilli really hot, increase chilli powder.

Fresh herbs are expensive to buy but cheap to grow; thyme is evergreen.

2lb (900g) herby pork sausages

1 tbsp oil

2 large onions, peeled

2 tsp mild chilli powder

1 tsp cumin seeds, roughly crushed

2 garlic cloves, crushed

2 tbsp plain flour

1 pt (600ml) chicken stock

1 tbsp caster sugar

3 tbsp tomato purée

2 × 14½oz (411g) cans red kidney beans

14½oz (411g) can cannellini beans

fresh thyme to garnish, optional

1 Preheat oven to 375°F, 190°C, Gas 5. Prick sausages. Heat oil in a large frying pan, add sausages and quickly brown over a high heat. Remove from pan with a draining spoon and transfer to a large casserole dish.

2 Slice onions, add to pan and fry, stirring occasionally until golden. Add chilli powder, cumin and garlic and cook for 1 minute. Stir in flour then add stock, sugar, tomato purée and seasoning.

3 Drain cans of beans and stir into casserole with stock mixture. Cover and cook for 1¼ hours. Garnish with thyme if liked and serve with jacket potatoes.

Jacket potatoes with yogurt or spiced butter

16 small baking potatoes – about 4¼lb (1.9kg), scrubbed

2tbsp oil

½ bunch spring onions, trimmed

6oz (150g) tub natural yogurt

1tsp coriander seeds, roughly crushed

¼tsp cumin seeds, roughly crushed

3oz (75g) butter

Crush coriander and cumin seeds using a pestle and mortar or put into a small bowl and crush with the end of a rolling pin.

1   Rub potatoes with a little oil and sprinkle with salt. Put in a roasting tin and cook above sausages for 1¼ hours or until tender.

2   Meanwhile, finely chop spring onions and stir into yogurt. Beat coriander and cumin seeds into butter. Chill until required.

3   Make a cross cut in top of each potato, spoon a little yogurt into 8 of the potatoes and sprinkle with coarsely ground black pepper. Add a knob of spiced butter to remaining potatoes. Offer one of each to serve.

Caramelised apple tart

PASTRY

8oz (225g) plain flour

4oz (100g) margarine

FILLING

2 eggs, size 3

3oz (75g) caster sugar

1 lemon, grated rind and juice

3 medium cooking apples – about 2lb (900g)

TOPPING

1oz (25g) margarine

1oz (25g) caster sugar

2tbsp marmalade

TO SERVE

1¾pt (1 litre) vanilla ice cream

Use a food processor if you have one to make pastry and to grate and slice apples.

You can substitute apricot jam for marmalade.

1   Put flour into a bowl with a pinch of salt. Cut margarine into pieces, add to flour and rub in with fingertips until fine crumbs form.

To freeze: cool completely then open freeze until solid. Remove tin, wrap in cling film, label and return to freezer. Use within 3 months. Defrost at room temperature.

Suitable for a vegetarian.

2 Mix to a smooth but not sticky dough with 3tbsp water. Knead lightly and roll out on a floured surface until a little larger than an 11in (28cm) loose-bottomed metal flan tin.

3 Lift pastry over a rolling pin, lay over tin then ease on to base and up sides pressing into place lightly with fingertips. Trim top and chill in fridge while making filling.

4 Preheat oven to 400°F, 200°C, Gas 6. Put eggs, sugar, lemon rind and juice in a bowl and mix with a fork.

5 Quarter, core and peel the apples; coarsely grate half of them. Stir grated apple into egg mixture then pour into pastry case. Spread into an even layer with the back of the spoon.

6 Thinly slice remaining apple quarters. Arrange, overlapping, over the top of the tart.

7 Melt margarine in a small saucepan or microwave on Full Power (100 per cent) for 30 seconds. Brush over apples then sprinkle with sugar.

8 Put tart on to a baking sheet and cook for 30 minutes.

9 Warm marmalade in a small saucepan or microwave on Full Power (100 per cent) for 30 seconds. Brush over apples then return to oven for 10–15 minutes more until caramelised and filling has set.

10 Serve warm with vanilla ice cream.

COUNTDOWN **In the morning**
Make tart or thaw if frozen. Scrub potatoes and place in tin. Make yogurt and spicy butter toppings.

2 hours before serving
Make sausage dish. Cook potatoes.

45 minutes before guests arrive
Prepare mulled wine.

Winter warming dinner for six

Spiced carrot soup

1 onion, peeled

2lb (900g) carrots, peeled

2oz (50g) margarine

1tsp cumin seeds, roughly crushed

1tsp coriander seeds, roughly crushed

2pt (1.1 litres) chicken stock

½pt (300ml) milk

Soup freezes well in a plastic box for up to 3 months. Freeze garnish in cling film or sprinkle soup with a little chopped fresh parsley.

1 Roughly chop onion and carrots. Heat margarine in a large saucepan, add vegetables, cover and fry for 10 minutes, stirring occasionally, until golden.

2 Add cumin and coriander seeds and cook for 1 minute then pour on stock and add plenty of salt and pepper.

3 Bring to boil, cover and simmer for 20 minutes until vegetables are tender. Reserve 2tbsp drained carrots for garnish.

4 Cool slightly then liquidise or process until smooth. Return to pan and stir in milk. Reheat when ready to serve.

5 Chop reserved carrots neatly, ladle soup into bowls and sprinkle with carrots.

Ready ground coriander and cumin can be used in place of whole seeds.

Decorate soup with swirls of natural yogurt or cream and 'feather' with a cocktail stick if liked.

Uses store cupboard ingredients.

You may prefer to remove bones before serving tagine.

Lamb may be cooked the day before and reheated thoroughly when required.

To freeze: cool lamb, pack into a plastic box. Cover and label. Freeze for up to 3 months.

Lamb tagine

2lb (900g) frozen stewing lamb, just thawed

1 onion

2 turnips

2 carrots

1in (2.5cm) piece fresh root ginger

1tbsp oil

1tsp ground cinnamon

1tsp coriander seeds, roughly crushed

4 cloves

1tbsp plain flour

1pt (600ml) lamb stock

1tbsp tomato purée

1oz (25g) currants

TO SERVE

12oz (325g) long grain rice

1tsp ground turmeric

2tbsp chopped parsley

1 Preheat oven to 350°F, 180°C, Gas 4. Trim excess fat away from lamb. Peel and coarsely chop onion, turnips and carrots. Peel and finely chop ginger.

2 Heat oil in a large frying pan, add lamb and fry over a high heat, turning occasionally, until browned on both sides. Lift out of pan and transfer to a casserole dish.

3 Fry onion, turnips and carrots for 5 minutes, stirring occasionally until lightly browned.

4 Stir in ginger, cinnamon, coriander, cloves and flour and cook for 1 minute. Stir in stock, tomato purée and currants. Bring to the boil then pour over lamb.

5 Cover casserole and transfer to the oven. Cook for 2 hours until lamb is tender.

6 Just before serving bring a saucepan of salted water to the boil, add rice and turmeric and cook for 8–10 minutes until rice is just tender. Drain, rinse with boiling water, drain again. Spoon into a dish. Serve lamb sprinkled with parsley.

Sticky walnut tart with orange custard

PASTRY

6oz (150g) plain flour

3oz (75g) margarine

FILLING

4oz (100g) walnut pieces

2oz (50g) margarine

6oz (150g) demerara sugar

8oz (225g) golden syrup

3 eggs, size 3

1 tsp vanilla essence

If you have a fan-assisted oven, cover top of tart loosely with foil after 20 minutes to keep nuts from burning.

Decorate top of tart by rerolling pastry trimmings and cutting out pretty shapes, or use miniature petits fours cutters.

Tart freezes well for up to 3 months overwrapped with foil.

1 Put flour into a bowl with a pinch of salt. Add margarine, cut into pieces, and rub in with fingertips until fine crumbs form.

2 Mix to a soft but not sticky dough with 2tbsp water. Knead lightly and roll out on a floured surface to a round a little larger than a 9in (23cm) loose-bottomed flan tin.

3 Lift pastry over rolling pin, transfer to flan tin and press on to base and up the sides using fingertips. Trim top and chill in fridge while making filling.

4 Put nuts, margarine, sugar and golden syrup into a saucepan and heat until margarine has melted and sugar has dissolved. Cool slightly.

5 Preheat oven to 375°F, 190°C, Gas 5. Beat eggs and vanilla essence together then gradually stir into nut mixture. Pour into flan case. Put tart on a baking sheet and cook for 35 minutes until just set in the centre.

6 Cool slightly then remove from tin and transfer to a serving plate. Serve with orange custard, see overleaf.

Stir 2tbsp sherry,
whisky or brandy into
finished custard

Quick to make.

Orange custard

2tbsp instant custard powder   ¾pt (450ml) milk

2tbsp caster sugar

1 orange, grated rind and juice

1 Mix custard powder, sugar, orange rind and juice together in a jug until smooth.

2 Bring milk just to the boil in a saucepan, whisk into orange mixture. Return to pan and bring back to the boil, whisking until thickened and smooth. Pour into a serving jug.

COUNTDOWN **2½ hours before serving**
Prepare and cook tagine on shelf just below centre of oven. Make tart and cook at 350°F, 180°C, Gas 4 on shelf above tagine. Make soup.

15 minutes before serving
Warm serving dishes and plates. Cook rice and keep hot. Make custard and keep hot with surface sprinkled with a little sugar so that no skin forms. Reheat soup. Cover tart with foil and reheat while eating main course.

Christmas drinks and nibbles party for eight

M E N U   *Parsnip and potato crisps with*
curried banana dip
Cheesy palmiers
Black olive and tomato crostini
Red spiced peanuts

Glühwein
Sparkling wine cup
Hot citrus tea

£££

Parsnip and potato crisps

1 lb (450g) parsnips, peeled
1 lb (450g) potatoes, peeled

18fl oz (½ litre) bottle sunflower oil

Beware of accidents when deep frying; never leave hot oil unattended.

Crisps can be made earlier in the day and reheated on a baking sheet in a hot oven 400°F, 200°C, Gas 6 for 5 minutes.

1 Cut vegetables into wafer-thin slices with a sharp knife or use slicer attachment on a food processor.

2 Pat dry with kitchen paper.

3 Heat oil in a large saucepan to 375°F, 190°C using a cooking thermometer, or until bubbles form immediately around a slice of potato dropped in to test. Cook potatoes and parsnips in small batches for 2–3 minutes until crisp and golden.

4 Lift out of oil with a draining spoon and drain well on kitchen paper. Sprinkle lightly with salt. Serve with curried banana dip.

Strain oil when cool and store in a screw-top jar for another time.

Keep surface of dip covered closely with cling film until required so no skin forms.

Best to use curry paste, which is sold in jars rather than curry powder which can give a raw taste to dips.

Curried banana dip

2 ripe bananas   ½tsp hot curry paste

6oz (150g) set natural yogurt

1 Mash bananas well then mix with yogurt and curry paste.

2 Spoon into a bowl and set on a large plate. Arrange potato and parsnip crisps around.

Palmiers can be made earlier in the day; reheat on low oven shelf for 5 minutes while reheating crisps, under crostini.

Pastry can also be spread with a little Marmite instead of mustard.

Cheesy palmiers

oil for greasing

1lb 2oz (500g) frozen puff pastry, just thawed

little flour for dusting work surface

2tsp Dijon mustard

1 egg, size 3, beaten

6oz (150g) Cheddar cheese, finely grated

1 small onion, finely chopped

1 Preheat oven to 425°F, 220°C, Gas 7. Lightly grease 2 baking sheets with a little oil.

2 Roll out half the pastry thinly on a lightly floured surface and cut into a rectangle 10 × 13in (25.5 × 33cm).

3 Brush with half the mustard and with beaten egg then sprinkle evenly with half the cheese and onion.

4 With a short edge near you, roll one long vertical side in towards the centre. Repeat with opposite side, rolling until both sides touch.

5 Brush outer edges of pastry with egg and cut roll crossways into thin slices. Place cut side uppermost on greased trays.

6 Cook for 8–10 minutes until well risen and golden. Remove from baking trays with a palette knife and transfer to a small basket for serving. Repeat with remaining ingredients.

Palmiers freeze well, packed into a plastic box and interleaved with greaseproof. Defrost for 1 hour then reheat in oven as described above.

Black olive and tomato crostini

6½oz (165g) can pitted black olives, drained

4tbsp oil

1 small French stick

2 garlic cloves, peeled and halved

2 tomatoes, chopped

1tbsp chopped fresh basil, marjoram or parsley

If buying olives from the delicatessen counter ask for 3oz (75g) pitted olives.

If French stick is large, halve slices so they are a convenient size to eat with the fingers.

1 Liquidise or process olives with 2tbsp oil until a coarse paste forms.

2 Cut bread into thin, nibble-sized slices and grill lightly on both sides. Rub over one side of each using the garlic cloves, put on to a baking sheet then drizzle with a little oil.

3 Divide olive mixture between bread slices and spread evenly. Top with tomatoes and herbs, and season well. Cover with cling film and set aside until ready to cook.

4 Preheat oven to 400°F, 200°C, Gas 6. Cook crostini for 10 minutes until piping hot then transfer to a serving plate.

Cool nuts and store in a screw-top jar for up to I week. Do not use a plastic box as the spices will discolour the plastic.

Choose peanuts without brown skins as they take on the colours of the spices better.

Red spiced peanuts

2tbsp oil

2 × 7oz (200g) bags shelled and skinned unsalted peanuts

3tsp paprika

I tsp cumin seeds, roughly crushed

I tsp ground turmeric

½ tsp salt

I Heat oil in a nonstick frying pan, add nuts and stir fry for 3–4 minutes until lightly browned.

2 Stir in spices and salt and fry for 1 minute, stirring until evenly coated in spices. Spoon into a dish and leave to cool.

Do not let wine boil or you will spoil the flavour. Serve hot but do not overheat or you risk guests burning their mouths.

Shop around for bargain prices — there is no need to use expensive wine in this recipe.

Add a little brandy if you have it.

Glühwein

MAKES 16 GLASSES

2 × 75cl bottles red wine

16 cloves

2 cinnamon sticks, halved

6oz (150g) caster sugar

I Put all ingredients into a saucepan with 2pt (1.1 litres) water. Bring slowly to the boil, stirring occasionally, until sugar has completely dissolved.

2 Take off heat and leave to stand for at least 1 hour for flavours to develop. Strain and return to pan.

3 When ready to serve, reheat but do not boil. Ladle into heatproof glasses.

Sparkling wine cup

MAKES 8 GLASSES
75cl bottle white wine
6tbsp sherry

1 orange, thinly sliced
½pt (300ml) fizzy lemonade

Add lemonade just before serving so that it doesn't go flat.

1 Put wine, sherry and orange into a large jug and chill in the fridge until required.

2 Add lemonade, stir and pour into glasses.

Choose an inexpensive fruity German wine.

Hot citrus tea

MAKES 12 GLASSES
4 breakfast tea bags
4tbsp clear honey

2tsp chopped glacé ginger
½pt (300ml) orange juice
1 lemon, thinly sliced

Quick to make.

1 Put tea bags into a jug with honey and ginger. Pour on 3pt (1.7 litres) boiling water. Stir in orange juice and leave to stand for 5 minutes.

Good for the drivers.

2 Remove tea bags and pour into heatproof glasses. Decorate with slices of lemon and serve immediately.

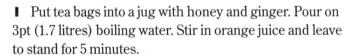

COUNTDOWN **In the morning**
Make all the nibbles, put nuts in a serving dish and set aside. Make glühwein and set aside. Chill bottles of white wine and lemonade.

30 minutes before serving
Mix white wine, sherry and orange slices together. Slowly reheat wine and set aside. Make curried banana dip. Reheat crips, crostini and palmiers. Make hot citrus tea.

Christmas Eve supper for four

M E N U

Bacon-wrapped trout
Tossed green salad
Sauté potatoes

££

Exotic fruit syllabub

Bacon-wrapped trout

For the best trout prices, try your local freezer centre.

Some guests may have difficulty coping with the bones. To bone fish before cooking, allow 30–40 minutes: insert a small knife into body cavity just behind head and sever backbone, being careful not to pierce flesh. Open out fish with one hand with skin downwards on chopping board, then loosen bones and peel away backbone. Sever backbone again just behind the tail.

4 frozen prepared trout, just thawed

½ lemon, juice only

8 rashers streaky bacon, rind removed

1 Rinse trout well with cold water. Arrange in the base of the grill pan, sprinkle lemon juice over and season.

2 Run a round-ended knife along length of each bacon rasher with light pressure to stretch until half as long again.

3 Wrap 2 rashers of bacon around each trout and secure with halved cocktail sticks.

4 Cook under a hot grill for 10 minutes, turning once until bacon is browned and fish flakes easily when pressed with a knife.

5 Remove cocktail sticks and put on to serving plates.

Tossed green salad

½ lemon, juice only

4tbsp oil

½tsp Dijon mustard

4½oz (115g) bag mixed salad leaves

Salads are always expensive at Christmas time; buying a bag of ready prepared salad means there is just the quantity needed with no wastage.

1 Whisk lemon juice, oil, mustard and seasoning together in the base of a salad bowl with a fork.

2 Wash salad leaves and tear into bite-sized pieces. Add to dressing just before serving and toss together.

Sauté potatoes

1¼lb (550g) potatoes, peeled   2–3tbsp oil

1 small onion, peeled

The large capacity of a wok makes it ideal for frying and tossing sauté potatoes.

1 Cut potatoes into large dice and cook in a saucepan of boiling salted water for 4–5 minutes until just tender.

2 Drain potatoes. Slice onion thinly.

Uses store cupboard ingredients.

3 Heat 2tbsp oil in a large frying pan, add potatoes, onion and seasoning and fry for 8–10 minutes, stirring frequently and adding more oil if needed, until browned and tender. Spoon into a serving bowl and serve with trout.

Exotic fruit syllabub

15oz (425g) can mango slices

1 passion fruit

½pt (300ml) whipping cream

2tbsp icing sugar

1 lemon, grated rind and 4tsp juice

4tbsp sherry, optional

Make no more than 2 hours in advance or cream will separate.

Canned mango is available from large supermarkets and specialist Indian supermarkets. If unavailable, use 1 large fresh mango instead. Stand mango on a chopping board and cut a thick slice off either side then cut flesh away from large central stone. Peel and slice and use as above.

1 Drain mangoes and halve slices, divide between 4 wine glasses. Halve passion fruit, scoop out seeds with a teaspoon and divide these between glasses.

2 Whip cream until peaking. Fold in icing sugar, lemon rind and juice then add sherry if using. Spoon on to fruit and chill until required.

Quick to make.

COUNTDOWN **In the morning**

Defrost trout. Stretch bacon rashers. Parboil potatoes. Prepare dressing.

40 minutes before serving

Make syllabub and chill. Wrap trout in bacon and grill. Fry potatoes. Wash salad and toss in dressing. Remove cocktail sticks from trout and serve main course.

Traditional Christmas lunch for eight

MENU

Roast turkey
Turkey gravy
Bread sauce
Fan roast potatoes
Brussels sprouts with bacon
Red cabbage with raisins
Peas

Christmas pudding
Sherried butter

£££   *Cinnamon mince pies*

Roast turkey

8–10lb (3.6–4.5kg) frozen turkey, thoroughly defrosted

1 onion, peeled

1 cooking apple, peeled and cored

1 tbsp oil

12oz (325g) pork sausagemeat

8oz (225g) fresh breadcrumbs

1 egg, size 3, beaten

2tbsp fresh chopped sage or 2tsp dried

2oz (50g) butter

TO GARNISH

8oz (225g) cocktail sausages

bunch fresh herbs, optional

For defrosting times follow instructions on turkey wrapper. Remove giblets as soon as possible.

If turkey is not cooked when tested, return to oven and test again 20 minutes later.

1 As soon as turkey is completely thawed, remove giblets and use for gravy (see following recipe). Rinse inside and outside of turkey with cold water, drain and pat dry with kitchen paper. Put on a plate.

Leaving cooked turkey to rest makes carving easier and frees oven for last minute cooking.

Garnishing with a bunch of fresh herbs covers unsightly leg stumps for party presentation so is worthwhile if you have plentiful supplies, but not if you have to buy specially.

Bought cranberry sauce is much cheaper than making your own.

2 Finely chop onion and apple. Heat oil in a frying pan, add onion and apple and fry for 5 minutes, stirring until softened. Cool then mix with sausagemeat, breadcrumbs, egg, sage and plenty of seasoning.

3 Preheat oven to 375°F, 190°C, Gas 5. Spoon half the stuffing into the neck end of the turkey then fold neck flap over stuffing and press into a good shape. Truss again if necessary.

4 Line a large roasting tin with 2 pieces of foil and put turkey in tin. Spread with butter and season. Bring foil up and over bird and twist edges to seal.

5 Shape remaining stuffing into small balls and put in a small roasting tin.

6 Roast turkey for 3½–4 hours, opening the foil for the last 30–40 minutes. To test the turkey, insert a small sharp knife into the thigh joint – juices will run clear when meat is cooked.

7 Reserving turkey cooking juices, transfer the turkey to a warmed serving plate and wrap tightly in foil. Leave to rest for 30 minutes. Make gravy, see following recipe.

8 Brush stuffing balls with a little turkey fat reserved from cooking juices and cook on top oven shelf for 30 minutes until browned. Put sausages in oven for last 15 minutes.

9 To serve, remove foil from turkey, arrange stuffing balls and sausages around it. Garnish with herbs, if liked.

Turkey gravy

turkey giblets	2 bay leaves
I onion, quartered	I tbsp cornflour
I carrot, quartered	

Add 4tbsp sherry, or red or white wine to gravy, if liked.

I Rinse giblets well and put into a saucepan with 2pt (1.1 litres) water, onion, carrot, bay leaves and seasoning.

2 Bring to boil, cover and simmer for 1½ hours.

3 Mix cornflour with a little cold water to form a smooth paste. Strain stock into cornflour and mix until smooth. Add more water to make up to 1¾pt (1 litre) with water if needed. Set aside until required.

Reheat gravy in gravy boat in the microwave, unless there is metallic decoration on it which would spark and blacken.

4 To finish, pour fat off turkey roasting juices, (retaining some for brushing stuffing balls), and pour turkey juices into a saucepan. Add stock mixture and bring to the boil, stirring. Cook for 5 minutes then pour into a warmed gravy boat.

Bread sauce

I onion	4oz (100g) fresh breadcrumbs
6 cloves	I oz (25g) butter
I pt (600ml) milk	4tbsp single cream
I bay leaf	

Make breadcrumbs in one large batch for stuffing and sauce.

Reheat in microwave in serving dish to save washing up.

I Spike onion with cloves and put in a saucepan with the milk and bay leaf. Bring to the boil and simmer gently for 10 minutes. Cool.

Sauce is best made on the day but breadcrumbs can be frozen in a plastic bag for up to 3 months. They can be used direct from the freezer, no need to allow thawing time.

2 Remove onion and bay leaf. Add breadcrumbs and seasoning and cook, stirring for 5 minutes, until thick. Stir in butter and cream. Cover surface with cling film if not serving immediately.

3 Reheat if needed, stirring frequently.

Fan roast potatoes

If potatoes are not brown enough when turkey is ready then brown quickly under a hot grill.

3lb (1.4kg) small baking potatoes, peeled

1oz (25g) butter

5tbsp oil

1 Cut thin slits in potatoes being careful not to cut right through. Parboil in a saucepan of boiling salted water for 5 minutes. Drain.

2 Heat butter and oil in a roasting tin on shelf above turkey for 5 minutes. Add potatoes, toss in butter and oil and roast on shelf above turkey for 1¼ hours.

3 Turn potatoes several times during cooking and transfer to base of oven when cooked. Drain and spoon into a warmed serving dish.

Brussels sprouts with bacon

Cook sprouts at the very last minute so they don't go soggy.

1½lb (675g) small Brussels sprouts
4oz (100g) streaky bacon, rind removed
2oz (50g) butter

1 Trim and peel outer leaves off sprouts. Halve any large ones.

2 Cook in a saucepan of boiling salted water for 10 minutes until just tender. Drain and dry pan.

3 Dry fry bacon in pan, stirring until browned. Add sprouts, butter and black pepper and toss together until butter has melted. Spoon into a warmed serving dish.

Red cabbage with raisins

I onion, peeled	¼pt (150ml) chicken stock
I¼lb (550g) red cabbage	2tbsp wine vinegar
I tbsp oil	2oz (50g) raisins
3 cloves	2tbsp cranberry sauce

Any remaining uncooked red cabbage will store in fridge for 10 days. Make into coleslaw (good with cold turkey) with a little chopped apple and grated carrot. Flavour with caraway seeds.

1 Finely chop onion. Thinly shred cabbage.

2 Heat oil in a saucepan add onion and fry for 5 minutes, stirring until softened. Add cabbage and cloves and cook for 3 minutes.

3 Add remaining ingredients and seasoning, cover and cook for 15–20 minutes, stirring occasionally, until cabbage is just soft.

Peas

I lb (450g) frozen peas

1 Cook in a saucepan of boiling salted water for 5 minutes. Drain and spoon into a warmed serving dish.

Cook in microwave if short of hob space.

Fruit soaked in tea rather than the traditional use of beer or fruit juice is much cheaper and tastes as good.

Christmas pudding is traditionally made months in advance and left to mature but this recipe can be made at the last minute — even the night before, if necessary.

To flame pudding, warm 3tbsp brandy in a small saucepan until almost boiling. Quickly pour over pudding and light with a match.

If putting coins into pudding, wrap in foil first.

Christmas pudding

oil for greasing

2lb (900g) mixed dried fruit

2oz (50g) glacé cherries, chopped

½pt (300ml) hot tea

3oz (75g) dark muscovado sugar

3oz (75g) shredded suet

3oz (75g) fresh breadcrumbs

2oz (50g) self-raising flour

1tsp ground cinnamon

2tbsp chopped glacé ginger

2 eggs, size 3, beaten

TO SERVE

sprig of holly

½pt (300ml) single cream

1 Grease a 2½pt (1.4 litre) pudding basin with a little oil and line base with a circle of greaseproof paper. Put dried fruit and cherries into a bowl, pour over hot tea and leave to soak for 2 hours.

2 Stir in remaining pudding ingredients and mix well. Spoon into basin and level top.

3 Cover pudding with a doubled piece of greaseproof paper, pleat top across centre and tie over basin with string. Add a large piece of pleated foil and tie securely with string. Add a string handle so pudding can be lifted out of pan easily.

4 Put an old saucer, inverted, in the base of a large saucepan. Stand pudding on saucer and pour in enough boiling water to come halfway up basin sides. Cover with lid and simmer for 3 hours, topping up water from time to time.

5 Leave to cool, then replace paper and foil coverings with fresh ones. Store in a cool place until required. To reheat, cook in saucepan as before for 2 hours.

6 Loosen edge of pudding and turn out on to a serving plate. Decorate with holly and serve with cream and sherried butter.

For vegetarians make sure you use vegetarian suet.

Cut down steam in the kitchen by using a pressure cooker or slow cooker, follow manual for timings.

Sherried butter

6oz (150g) unsalted butter

12oz (325g) icing sugar

4tbsp sherry

Use butter at room temperature for easy mixing.

Beat all ingredients together in a food processor if you have one.

1 Put butter into a bowl and gradually beat in icing sugar and sherry alternately. Beat until smooth and soft.

2 Spoon into a bowl, cover loosely with cling film and chill until required.

Use a miniature bottle of brandy or rum if preferred.

To freeze: spoon into a plastic box. Seal, label and freeze for up to 3 months. Defrost for 3 hours at room temperature.

Cinnamon mince pies

12oz (325g) plain flour

1½tsp ground cinnamon

6oz (150g) margarine

14½oz (411g) jar mincemeat

1 egg, size 3, beaten to glaze

2tbsp caster sugar

To freeze: cool completely then pack into a plastic box. Seal, label and freeze for up to 3 months. Thaw for 3 hours at room temperature then warm in oven.

1 Preheat oven to 375°F, 190°C, Gas 5. Put flour and 1tsp cinnamon in a bowl. Add margarine and rub in with fingertips until fine crumbs form.

Best served warm so
sherried butter melts
through slits in tops
of pies.

Block or soft
margarine or butter
may be used.

2 Stir in 4tbsp cold water and mix to a smooth dough. Knead lightly and roll out on a floured surface. Stamp out 16, 3in (7.5cm) circles with a fluted biscuit cutter, re-rolling pastry as needed. Press circles into sections of 2 bun trays.

3 Spoon mincemeat into cases and dampen edges of pastry with a little beaten egg.

4 Roll out remaining pastry and trimmings and cut 16, 2½in (6.5cm) circles with a fluted biscuit cutter. Position over mincemeat and press edges together well. Make 3 tiny slits in top of each pie then brush with egg.

5 Mix remaining ½tsp cinnamon and caster sugar together and sprinkle over pies. Cook for 20 minutes until browned. Cool slightly in tin then loosen with a knife and serve warm or cold with sherried butter.

COUNTDOWN **One month before**
Make Christmas pudding. Make and freeze mince pies, sherried butter, breadcrumbs for bread sauce. Buy frozen turkey.

2 days before Christmas
Defrost turkey. Check that table linen is clean, iron if needed. Make table decoration and name cards if liked. Make mince pies if not already made and store in tin if freezer is full.

Christmas Eve
Wash turkey and put on a large plate, wrap loosely and store in fridge. Make stuffing but do not put in turkey. Make giblet stock for gravy. Prepare sprouts and shred cabbage, store in separate plastic bags in the fridge. Make sherried butter, and breadcrumbs for bread sauce if not already made. Lay the table if not using for breakfast.

Christmas Day 9.15am
Preheat oven to 375°F, 190°C, Gas 5. Stuff turkey and put on to roast at 9.45am. Thaw mince pies and sherried butter.

COUNTDOWN **Christmas Day 9.15am continued**

Parboil potatoes and set aside. Chop onion for red cabbage recipe. Cook onion in milk for bread sauce.

12pm

Reheat Christmas pudding.

12.45pm

Open foil around turkey so it can brown. Roast potatoes.

1.15pm

Test turkey, if not cooked return to oven loosely wrapped in foil. Top up water in pudding pan if necessary. Cook stuffing balls. Warm plates, serving dishes and turkey plate, in oven if free, or by putting plates in a bowl of hot water and pouring hot water into vegetable dishes.

Cook sausages. Transfer cooked turkey to serving plate and wrap tightly in foil. Put potatoes in a serving dish back in the oven. Cook cabbage. Finish bread sauce and gravy. Fry bacon, cook peas. Cook and finish sprouts at the last minute.

2pm

Serve lunch. Put mince pies on a baking sheet and warm through in turned-off oven while eating main course. Turn out pudding and flame, if liked, just before serving.

New Year's Eve dinner for six

M E N U   *Warm leek mousses with melba toast*

Poulet au Noël
Potatoes dauphinoises

££   *Caramelised clementines with gingered fromage frais*

Warm leek mousses

Buy vegetables from your local street market for best prices, watching out for good quality.

Mousses will rise in oven but sink down again on cooling. Make breadcrumbs in processor or liquidiser before adding sliced leeks and remaining ingredients.

Suitable for a vegetarian.

1½lb (675g) leeks, trimmed

oil for greasing

1oz (25g) margarine

1oz (25g) fresh breadcrumbs

3 eggs, size 3

¼pt (150ml) milk

generous pinch grated nutmeg

TO GARNISH

2 tomatoes

½ bunch watercress, optional

1 Peel off outer layers from the leeks to give ten 'leaves', wash well and reserve. Thinly slice remaining leeks and wash well.

2 Blanch leek leaves in a large saucepan of boiling water for 2 minutes. Drain, rinse with cold water and drain again.

3 Brush 6 ramekin dishes with a little oil. Cut leaves into thin 5in (12.5cm) lengths and use to line ramekins, arranging like spokes of a wheel. Fill in any gaps with oddments.

4 Dry pan, heat margarine and fry sliced leeks for 5 minutes until softened but not browned. Cool slightly.

5 Process or liquidise cooked leeks with the breadcrumbs, eggs, milk and nutmeg and pour into the ramekin dishes. Fold overhanging leek strips over the top then put dishes in a roasting tin. Chill until required.

6 Preheat oven to 350°F, 180°C, Gas 4. Pour in enough boiling water to come halfway up sides of dishes. Cover tin loosely with foil and cook on shelf below chicken for 45–60 minutes until mousses are set.

7 Meanwhile, remove any green tops from tomatoes and cut a cross in the base of each. Put into a bowl, cover with boiling water and leave for 30 seconds. Drain, peel away skin then finely chop tomatoes discarding seeds. Reserve for garnish.

8 Cool mousses slightly then loosen all around each rim with a knife. Turn out on to individual serving plates. Reserve a little watercress for garnishing main course, if using; tear remaining watercress into tiny sprigs and arrange sprigs around mousses alternating with chopped tomato. Serve with melba toast.

Melba toast

6 medium thick slices white bread

1 Lightly toast bread on both sides. Trim off crusts.

2 Cut each piece of toast through centre to make 2 very thin slices. Then cut into small triangles. Place on a baking sheet, uncooked side upwards, cover tightly with cling film to prevent drying out and set aside until needed.

3 Cook under a hot grill until curled and lightly browned.

Can also serve with pâté or prawn cocktail.

Turns ordinary toast into a party accompaniment.

Poulet au Noël

Buy large bags of frozen chicken thighs from the freezer centre for lowest prices.

Look out for wine on special offer in freezer centres or in the supermarket ideally choosing a well flavoured wine, such as Burgundy.

Substitute a roasting tin for large casserole and cover top tightly with foil.

Casserole may be made the day before if preferred and kept chilled; always ensure chicken dishes are reheated thoroughly.

2 small onions, peeled

4oz (100g) streaky bacon, rind removed

8oz (225g) fresh chestnuts

12 frozen chicken thighs, just thawed

1oz (25g) margarine

2tbsp oil

2 garlic cloves, crushed

2tbsp plain flour

¼pt (150ml) cheap red wine

½pt (300ml) chicken stock

1tsp mixed dried herbs

4oz (100g) stoned prunes

TO SERVE

1lb (450g) Brussels sprouts

watercress sprigs to garnish, optional

1 Preheat oven to 350°F, 180°C, Gas 4. Thinly slice onions and chop bacon. Using a strong small knife, cut a cross in base of chestnuts and cook in a saucepan of boiling water for 5 minutes. Drain, cool slightly then peel off skins using the knife as necessary.

2 Trim skin on chicken thighs for a neat appearance.

3 Heat margarine and oil in a large frying pan. Fry chicken in batches until browned on both sides. Drain and transfer to a large casserole dish.

4 Add onions and bacon to pan and fry until browned. Add garlic and cook for 1 minute. Stir in flour then gradually add wine and stock. Add herbs and seasoning and bring to the boil, stirring.

5 Pour over chicken, add chestnuts and prunes; cover and cook for 1½ hours.

6 Trim and halve any large sprouts. Cook in boiling salted water for 5 minutes just before serving chicken. Drain and transfer sprouts to a warmed serving dish.

7 Put chicken on to a warmed serving plate with a little of the sauce. Garnish with watercress if using and serve remaining sauce in a gravy boat.

Potatoes dauphinoises

2lb (900g) potatoes, peeled

2tsp cornflour

2 garlic cloves, crushed

½pt (300ml) milk

½oz (15g) margarine

Sprinkle potato layers with 2oz (50g) grated Cheddar cheese if liked.

1 Thinly slice potatoes. Cook in a large saucepan of boiling salted water for 3 minutes until almost tender. Drain well.

2 Layer potatoes in a shallow ovenproof dish, seasoning each layer.

Any leftover potatoes dauphinoises reheats well in the microwave.

3 Put cornflour and garlic in a bowl and mix to a smooth paste with a little milk. Stir in remaining milk. Pour over potatoes. Dot with margarine and set aside until ready to cook.

4 Cook on shelf above chicken at 350°F, 180°C, Gas 4 for 1 hour until browned.

Uses store cupboard ingredients.

Caramelised clementines

12 clementines

2tbsp chopped glacé ginger

8oz (225g) granulated sugar

7oz (200g) fromage frais

few sprigs fresh rosemary to decorate, optional

Look out for ready chopped glacé ginger alongside the dried fruit in the supermarket; it is much cheaper than stem ginger or crystallised ginger.

1 Peel clementines and leave whole, put into a glass serving dish with 1tbsp of the ginger.

2 Put sugar and ¼pt (150ml) water into a heavy-based saucepan. Bring to the boil slowly without stirring until sugar has dissolved. Boil rapidly for about 10 minutes until just beginning to turn pale golden.

Do not stir the sugar syrup or it is likely to crystallise.

3 Remove from heat Add 4fl oz (120ml) boiling water, at arm's length as syrup will spit. Tilt pan to mix. Cool slightly then pour over clementines. Leave to cool completely.

Substitute fresh bay leaves for the rosemary or choose clementines sold with their leaves.

4 Reserve a little of the remaining ginger for decoration and stir remainder into fromage frais. Spoon into a serving dish and sprinkle with reserved ginger. Decorate clementines with sprigs of rosemary just before serving, if liked.

COUNTDOWN **In the morning**

Make caramelised clementines. Prepare ingredients for main course: slice onion, dice bacon, peel chestnuts. Make triangles of bread for melba toast, cover with cling film and set aside.

In the afternoon

Make mousses but do not cook. Skin tomatoes and chop. Chill until required.

2 hours before serving

Make chicken casserole. Put casserole and mousses in oven at same time and cook casserole on shelf above centre of oven with mousses below. Cook mousses for 30 minutes then transfer to base of oven for 15–30 minutes to finish cooking. Make potatoes dauphinoises. Transfer chicken to lower oven shelf and cook potatoes on shelf above for 1 hour. Warm plates and dishes for main course.

Just before serving

Toast second side of melba toast. Turn out mousses and garnish. Turn oven off and put a saucepan of water on to boil for sprouts. Cook sprouts while clearing starter plates.

About Age Concern

Entertaining on a Budget is one of a wide range of publications produced by Age Concern England, the National Council on Ageing. Age Concern England is actively engaged in training, information provision, fundraising and campaigning for retired people and those who work with them, and also in the provision of products and services such as insurance for older people.

A network of over 1,400 local Age Concern groups, with the support of around 250,000 volunteers, aims to improve the quality of life for older people and develop services appropriate to local needs and resources. These include advice and information, day care, visiting services, transport schemes, clubs, and specialist facilities for older people who are physically and mentally frail.

Age Concern England is a registered charity dependent on public support for the continuation and development of its work.

Age Concern England
1268 London Road
London SW16 4ER
Tel: 081-679 8000

Age Concern Cymru
4th Floor
1 Cathedral Road
Cardiff CF1 9SD
Tel: 0222 371566

Age Concern Scotland
54a Fountainbridge
Edinburgh EH3 9PT
Tel: 031-228 5656

Age Concern Northern Ireland
3 Lower Crescent
Belfast BT7 1NR
Tel: 0232 245729

Publications from ◆A◆C◆E◆ Books

A wide range of titles is published by Age Concern England under the ACE Books imprint.

Money Matters

The Pensions Handbook: A mid-life guide to improving retirement income

Jennie Hawthorne with Sue Ward

Many older people in their later working lives become concerned about the adequacy of their existing pension arrangements. This title addresses these worries and suggests strategies via which the value of a prospective pension can be enhanced. Advice is also provided on monitoring company pension schemes.

£5.95 0–86242–124–1

Your Rights: A guide to money benefits for older people

Sally West

A highly acclaimed annual guide to the State benefits available to older people. Contains current information on income support, housing benefit, council tax benefit and retirement pensions, among other sources of financial help, and includes advice on how to claim them.

For further information, please telephone 081-679 8000.

Your Taxes and Savings: A guide for older people
Sally West and Jennie Hawthorne

This annually updated guide explains how the tax system affects people over retirement age, including how to avoid paying more tax than necessary. The information about savings covers the wide range of investment opportunities now available.

For further information, please telephone 081-679 8000.

The Insurance Handbook: A guide for older people
Wayne Asher

Older people have particular needs – and opportunities – when purchasing insurance. This practical guide provides a handy overview of the products on the market, including home, car, health and life insurance, and helps readers make an informed choice.

£6.95   0–86242–146–2

Health and Care

A Warden's Guide to Health Care in Sheltered Housing
Dr Anne Roberts

The new edition of this invaluable guide examines the role of the warden and contains the key information all wardens should know about the health needs of older people. Practical advice on the best means of promoting better health among residents and providing emergency care is also included.

£13.95   0–86242–113–6

CareFully: A guide for home care assistants
Lesley Bell

Recent legislation places increasing emphasis on the delivery of care to older people in their own homes, thereby underling the crucial role of home care assistants. This accessible guide provides practical advice on the day-to-day tasks encountered and addresses such issues as legal responsibilities and emotional involvement.

£9.95   0–86242–129–2

General

Eating Well on a Budget
Sara Lewis

Completely revised, the new edition of this successful title offers sound advice on shopping and cooking cost-effectively and includes wholesome original recipies for four complete weekly menus,
£5.95 0–86242–120–9

An Active Retirement
Nancy Tuft

Bursting with information on hobbies, sports, educational opportunities and voluntary work, this practical guide is ideal for retired people seeking new ways to fill their time but uncertain where to start.
£7.95 0–86242–119–5

Your Retirement
Caroline Hartnell

A comprehensive handbook for older people leaving employment and looking ahead to retirement. Full of practical advice to assist with planning and adjustment, topics covered include: managing money, using your time, staying healthy, housing and special needs.
£4.95 0–86242–144–6

To order books, please send a cheque or money order made payable to Age Concern England to the address below. Postage and packing are free. Credit card orders may be made on 081-679 8000.

Age Concern England (DEPT ENT)
PO Box 9
London SW16 4EX

Information factsheets

Age Concern England produces over 30 factsheets on a variety of subjects.

To ORDER FACTSHEETS

Single copies are available free on receipt of a 9″ × 6″ sae. If you require a selection of factsheets or multiple copies totalling more than five, charges will be given on request.

A complete set of factsheets is available in a ring binder at the current cost of £34, which includes the first year's subscription. The current cost for annual subscription for subsequent years is £15. There are different rates of subscription for people living abroad.

Factsheets are revised and updated throughout the year and membership of the subscription service will ensure that your information is always current.

For further information, or to order factsheets, write to:

Information and Policy Department
Age Concern England
1268 London Road
London SW16 4ER

Index to the recipes

antipasto platter 40
apple and cumin stuffing 44
apple sauce 45
avocados, warm bacon and, salad 63

bacon
    bacon-wrapped trout 112
    Brussels sprouts with bacon 118–119
    chicken parcels 82
    cockles in parsley sauce 95
    Poulet au Noël 126
    sausage wraps 59
    warm bacon and avocado salad 63
banana dip, curried 108
bangers and mash with beery onion gravy 96
beef
    sizzling steak with noodles 32–33
    spicy beef samosas 35–36
black olive and tomato crostini 109
bread, hot herb 75–76
bread sauce 117–118
broccoli, cauliflower and 72
Brussels sprouts 126
    with bacon 118–119
butter, sherried 121

cabbage
    leaves, stuffed 55
    red with raisins 119
    stir-fried 46
caramelised apple tart 101–102
caramelised clementines 127–128
carrots
    carrot and sunflower seed salad 78
    gingered 46
    glazed carrots and turnips 92
    purée 71

spiced carrot soup 103
cauliflower and broccoli 72
celery and Stilton soup 69
cheat's yogurt brulée 65
cheesy palmiers 108–109
chicken
    chicken parcels 82
    chicken stir-fry 31–32
    lemony roast chicken 90–91
    Poulet au Noël 126
    Southern-style chicken 81
    warm chicken liver salad 26
chilled cucumber soup 21
chillied bangers and beans 100
chocolate
    chocolate brownies 79–80
    chocolate orange truffle cake 52–53
    creamy chocolate truffles 15–16
    hot chocolate sauce 28–29
Christmas pudding 120–121
chunky tomato soup with pesto croutons 89–90
cinnamon mince pies 121–122
citrus salad 60
cockles in parsley sauce 95
creamy chocolate truffles 15–16
crème caramel 87–88
croutons 89–90
curried banana dip 108

drinks
    Glühwein 110
    hot citrus tea 111
    mulled win 99
    sparkling wine cup 111
duchesse potatoes 51–52

egg-fried rice 32
exotic fruit syllabub 114

fan roast potatoes 118
fish and seafood
    bacon-wrapped trout 112
    cockles in parsley sauce 95
    Normandy mussels 27
French onion soup 85
French-style peas 92
fruit
    apple and cumin stuffing 44
    apple sauce 45
    curried banana dip 108
    mint and apple raita 36
    minted melon cocktail 74
    see also pastry; puddings and desserts;
    salads

Gateau Paris-Brest with hot chocolate sauce
28–29
gingered carrots 46
glazed carrots and turnips 92
Glühwein 110
gnocchi, potato, with tomato sauce 86–87
gourmet rice pudding 62
gravy, turkey 116

hash browns 59
herby new potatoes 83
honeyed noisettes of lamb with rosemary 22
hot bean salad 23
hot cheese soufflés 49–50
hot citrus tea 111
hot herb bread 75
hummus 54

jacket potatoes with yogurt or spiced butter
101

kulfi 38

lamb
    honeyed noisettes of lamb with rosemary
    22
    lamb and kidney bean pie 50–51
    lamb tagine 104
    stuffed cabbage leaves 55
leek mousses, warm 124
lemon meringue pie 47
lemony roast chicken 90–91

mackerel and potato salad with horseradish
dressing 75
Mediterranean vegetables with couscous 67
Melba toast 125
mint and apple raita 36
minted melon cocktail 74
minted strawberry and kiwi salad 68
mulled wine 99
mushroom strudel with sherry sauce 70–71

Normandy mussels 27

pancake rolls 30–31
pasta
    pesto and penne 64
    tagliatelle with spinach and mushrooms
    41
pastry
    baklava 56
    caramelised apple tart 101–102
    cheesy palmiers 108–109
    cinnamon mince pies 121–122
    mushroom strudel with sherry sauce
    70–71
    raised pork pie 77–78
    spicy beef samosas 35–36
    sticky walnut tart with orange custard
    105
    tomato tarts 66
peas 92, 119
pesto and penne 64
plum and cinnamon meringue gateau 93
pork
    pork and chorizo hotpot 61–62
    raised pork pie 77–78
    roast pork with mustard and honey
    crackling 43–44
potatoes
    bangers and mash with beery onion
    gravy 96
    celery and Stilton soup 69
    dauphinoises 127
    duchesse 51–52
    fan roast 118
    gnocchi with tomato sauce 86–87
    hash browns 59
    herby new 83
    jacket with yogurt or spiced butter 101
    mackerel and potato salad with
    horseradish dressing 75
    parsnip and potato crisps 107
    roast with thyme 91
    salad 79

sauté 113
-sesame 23
spicy roast and parsnips 45

Poulet au Noël 126

puddings and desserts
caramelised clementines 127–128
cheat's yogurt brulée 65
chocolate orange truffle cake 52–53
Christmas pudding 120–121
crème caramel 87–88
exotic fruit syllabub 114
Gateau Paris-Brest with hot chocolate sauce 28–29
gourmet rice pudding 62
kulfi 38
lemon meringue pie 47
peach and macaroon crush 76
plum and cinnamon meringue gateau 93
rhubarb sorbet 72–73
strawberry shortcakes 24
sultana syrup sponge 97
tiramisu 42
toffee bananas 33–34
see also pastry

raised pork pie 77–78

raita, mint and apple 36

red cabbage with raisins 119

red spiced peanuts 110

rhubarb sorbet 72–73

rice
egg-fried rice 32
gourmet rice pudding 62

roast pork with mustard and honey crackling 43–44

roast potatoes with thyme 91

roast turkey 115–116

salads
caramelised fruit 84
carrot and sunflower seed 78
citrus 60
hot bean 23
mackerel and potato with horseradish dressing 75
minted strawberry and kiwi 68
potato 79
tossed green 83, 113
warm bacon and avocado 63
warm chicken liver 26

sausages
bangers and mash with beery onion gravy 96
chillied bangers and beans 100
pork and chorizo hotpot 61–62

with roast turkey 115–116
sausage wraps 59

sauté potatoes 113

sesame potatoes 23

sherried butter 121

sizzling steak with noodles 32–33

sorbet, rhubarb 72–73

soufflé-stuffed tomatoes 58

soufflés, hot cheese 49–50

soup
celery and Stilton 69
chilled cucumber 21
chunky tomato with pesto croutons 89–90
French onion 85
spiced carrot 103

Southern-style chicken 81

sparkling wine cup 111

spiced carrot soup 103

spicy beef samosas 35–36

spicy roast potatoes and parsnips 45

spinach dhansak 37

sticky walnut tart with orange custard 105

stir-fried cabbage 46

strawberry and kiwi salad, minted 68

strawberry shortcakes 24

stuffed cabbage leaves 55

stuffing, apple and cumin 44

sultana syrup sponge 97

tagliatelle with spinach and mushrooms 41

tea, hot citrus 111

tiramisu 42

toffee bananas 33–34

tomato soup, chunky, with pesto croutons 89–90

tomato tarts 66

tomatoes, soufflé-stuffed 58

tossed green salad 83, 113

trout, bacon-wrapped 112

turkey, roast 115–116

turnips, glazed carrots and 92

warm bacon and avocado salad 63

warm leek mousses 124

yogurt brulée, cheat's 65